Your

COMPETITIVE
ADVANTAGE

AN ATHLETE'S GUIDE TO GETTING
HIRED AFTER SPORTS

Dr. Armin McCrea-Dastur

Story **BUILDERS** P R E S S

CONTENTS

PREFACE

You've spent years pushing your physical and mental limits, striving for excellence, and learning the value of teamwork, discipline, and perseverance. But everything you've gained through sports goes far beyond the game. You've built a mindset and a skill set that can carry you to success in every aspect of life—including your career. Stepping off the playing field and into the professional world might feel overwhelming at first. But here's the truth: you already have what it takes to thrive.

This book was written specifically for you—for athletes and former athletes who are ready to bring the skills, habits, and experiences from sport into the business world. The competitive spirit, work ethic, and mental toughness you developed during your athletic career aren't just impressive. They're powerful. When you understand how to use them, those traits can make you stand out in any industry. This book will help you translate what you've already built into something even bigger: a fulfilling, high-impact career.

The idea for this book came from a conversation with a former collegiate athlete—someone smart, driven, and experienced under pressure. They said, "I just don't know how to talk about what I bring to the table. I don't have any job experience. All I've ever done is compete." That moment stuck with me. Not because it was rare—but because it was so common. I've heard versions of that statement again and again from athletes who've trained, led, sacrificed, adapted, and performed at the highest levels—yet feel unsure of how to tell their story outside of sport.

And I realized: no one's helping you connect the dots.

I've spent decades working at the highest levels of Human Resources—leading talent development, coaching executives, and designing hiring systems for Fortune 500 companies across industries like healthcare, retail, consumer products, and more. I've sat in the rooms where career-making decisions are made. I know what hiring managers are looking for. I've trained them to identify leadership, recognize potential, and understand what real high performance looks like. But I've also seen the gap between what organizations need—and how athletes are taught to present themselves.

I know that gap well because I've lived at the intersection of both worlds. Before stepping into corporate leadership, I spent ten years with the University of North Carolina men's basketball program, including the 2005 national championship season. I wasn't just observing high performance—I was surrounded by it. I learned firsthand what it means to prepare, to lead, and to deliver under pressure. I saw how championship cultures are built: through clarity, accountability, focus, and mental toughness.

I've also been in your shoes. As a former competitive figure skater and a sport psychology consultant, I've studied the inner architecture of high performance. I've worked with athletes one-on-one, and I've lived through the discipline, the doubt, the pressure, and the pursuit. But what's driven me more than anything is helping athletes not just perform—but grow into who they're meant to be when the game ends.

2

Because here's the hard truth: too often, athletes are left out of the career conversation once their playing days are over. You're told to "start over." But the reality is, you're already ahead. You've built habits, mindsets, and leadership experiences that most professionals never touch. The only missing piece is learning how to speak their value—and that's exactly what this book is here to help you do.

This is your roadmap. A practical guide to help you take the excellence you built through sport and apply it to every step of your professional journey. This is about turning everything you already are into everything you want to become.

Each chapter focuses on a core skill you've likely developed as an athlete—and shows how it applies to both sport and business. You'll learn how to:

→ Use **discipline** to stay focused and committed in your new career

→ Manage your **time** efficiently to balance professional and personal demands

→ Apply **strategic thinking** to analyze challenges and make effective decisions

→ **Communicate** effectively to get your ideas heard and build strong relationships

→ Harness **leadership** to inspire teams and guide others toward success

→ Thrive in a **teamwork** environment where collaboration is key

→ Cultivate **emotional intelligence** to understand and manage emotions

→ Channel your **competitive drive and work ethic** to improve and strive for excellence

→ Stay **adaptable and coachable** in the face of change

→ Leverage **resilience** to bounce back from setbacks and keep pushing forward

Along the way, you'll get practical tools. This book will help you write a résumé that highlights your athletic experience and strengths. You'll learn how to prepare for interviews that showcase your potential—and make hiring managers see you as someone who's ready to contribute and lead.

Whether you're a student-athlete stepping into your first job or a seasoned competitor making a career shift, this book is here to support you. You have everything you need to succeed in the business world. Your athletic career was just the beginning. The habits, mindset, and grit that brought you success before will take you even further now.

This is your next chapter. Let's get to work.

THE BRIDGE BETWEEN SPORTS
AND CORPORATE SUCCESS

For years, you may have been conditioned to believe that your skills were limited to the playing field. That the discipline, leadership, teamwork, and grit you developed through sport were only useful in games, matches, or competitions. But that couldn't be further from the truth. The same qualities that made you successful as an athlete are exactly what make you valuable in the workplace. The transition from sports to business isn't just possible, it's a natural progression.

The moment you step off the field, court, track, pool, or rink for the last time, you might feel a mix of emotions: pride, uncertainty, excitement, even fear of the unknown. That's normal. But here's the truth: your journey is far from over. Everything you've endured, fought for, and achieved as an athlete has been preparing you for this next chapter. The same fire that fueled your early-morning workouts, helped you push through brutal losses, and drove your comebacks is the same fire that will fuel your success in your career.

This book is here to help you recognize the true value of your athletic experience and use it to build a career with purpose, impact, and growth. Whether you're stepping away from sport right now or just beginning to think about what comes next, you're not starting over. You're stepping forward with skills, habits, and experiences that are already shaping you into a future leader.

The reality is, only a small percentage of athletes go on to play professionally. But 100% of athletes enter the workforce in some capacity. And far too many don't realize the advantages they hold over their non-athlete peers. You've developed discipline, resilience, leadership, and adaptability—the exact qualities companies are desperate to find. These are the traits that turn new hires into top performers, and teammates into managers, directors, and executives.

The challenge isn't that you don't have what it takes. The challenge is that no one's ever shown you how to talk about what you bring to the table. You might assume your value ended when your athletic career did. That couldn't be more wrong. You are more than your stats, records, or championships. You are a powerhouse of transferable skills, sharpened through years of competitive experience, skills that can make you an asset in any industry.

Companies are constantly searching for people who know how to perform under pressure, collaborate with a team, bounce back from setbacks, and stay focused on results. That's your wheelhouse. You already have what so many employers are looking for. In fact, I've had executives tell me they would rather hire someone with raw athletic talent and a coachable mindset than someone with years of traditional experience but bad habits. You're not behind, you're exactly what many organizations need.

So don't look at graduation or retirement from sport as the end of your competitive journey. See it as a transformation, a shift from one arena to another. In the business world, success still comes down to strategy, execution, teamwork, and perseverance. The only difference is the scoreboard. You're still competing. You're still pushing to win. You're just playing a new game.

Let's get started.

THE TRANSFERABLE SKILLS OF ATHLETES

Think about the core skills that define an athlete:

- → **Commitment to Excellence**—The ability to set goals, work hard, and improve over time.

- → **Time Management**—Balancing practice, academics, and personal life requires an exceptional level of organization and efficiency.

- → **Resilience**—Facing challenges, overcoming injuries, and pushing through adversity are part of an athlete's DNA.

→ **Coachability**—Adjusting to new coaches, teammates, game plans, and unexpected challenges mirrors the corporate world's need for flexibility.

→ **Leadership & Teamwork**—Whether leading by example or working within a group, these skills translate seamlessly into corporate culture.

The playing field and the boardroom have more in common than you might think. The same hunger that drives you as an athlete to wake up before sunrise to train is the same hunger that fuels you as a top executive to push through setbacks and innovate in business. The same focus that allows you to drown out the noise of a hostile crowd is the same focus that will allow you to thrive under pressure in high-stakes meetings.

For instance, Phil Knight's success in building Nike wasn't just luck or timing. It was forged on the track at the University of Oregon, where his experience as a middle-distance runner taught him the discipline, grit, and mindset needed to conquer far bigger challenges. His discipline as a runner fueled his tireless work ethic, making long hours and repeated failures feel like just another part of the process. When his business faced near-collapse, Knight's resilience kept him moving forward, much like pushing through the final painful stretch of a race. As Knight himself reflected, "The art of competing, I'd learned from track, was the art of forgetting... You must forget your limits. You must forget your doubts, your pain... You must forget that internal voice screaming, begging, 'Not one more step.'" Nike's rise wasn't just because of shoes, it was the athlete's mindset, applied relentlessly to business, that turned a small idea into a global powerhouse.

Many of the most successful business leaders today were once athletes. They credit their corporate achievements to the same attributes that made them great competitors. Whether you aspire to be an entrepreneur, a corporate executive, or a high-performing employee, the lessons you've learned through sports will serve as a foundation for success.

YOUR PLAYBOOK FOR THE NEXT CHAPTER

This book is structured to guide you through the transition from athlete to corporate professional.

→ **Chapter 3 and Beyond**—We dive deep into the core competencies that make athletes ideal employees and leaders. Each chapter explores a specific skill, how it was developed through sports, and how it applies in business.

→ **Real-World Application**—Every concept is paired with actionable advice, including how to articulate your athletic experience on a resume, in interviews, and in networking settings.

→ **Success Stories**—Throughout the book, you will find real-life examples of former athletes who successfully leveraged their skills to excel in corporate America.

This book isn't just about finding a job. It's about recognizing your worth, owning your strengths, and confidently stepping into your next challenge. You have already proven yourself in one of the most demanding environments possible: sports. Now, it's time to take that same passion and energy and channel it into a career that excites and fulfills you.

▓▓ Postgame Recap

As an athlete, you have spent years cultivating discipline, mental toughness, and a relentless drive for success. These are not just traits of great competitors, they are the hallmarks of great professionals. Your experiences have uniquely prepared you for the challenges and opportunities of the corporate world.

The goal of this book is to help you recognize, embrace, and capitalize on the skills you already possess. By the time you finish, you will not only see yourself as an athlete but also as a valuable asset in the professional world, one that corporate America is actively looking for.

Your career is another game to be played, another challenge to be conquered. And just like in sports, the ones who succeed are those who are willing to put in the work, adapt, and never back down from a challenge. You are not starting from zero. You are starting from a position of strength.

Now, let's get to work.

2

TOP SKILLS CORPORATE LEADERS LOOK FOR IN CANDIDATES

I n the competitive world of corporate America, hiring managers are constantly searching for people who can drive results, foster innovation, and lead teams effectively. Yes, technical knowledge and job-specific skills matter, but the most sought-after qualities go beyond what can be learned in a textbook. They're the same attributes you've been building through sport: resilience, leadership, discipline, and teamwork.

Realizing this is a game-changer. You haven't just been playing a sport. You've been developing a mindset, a way of thinking and performing, that gives you an edge in the professional world. Every grueling practice, every setback you've bounced back from, every time you pushed past your limits, that's been shaping you into exactly the kind of person companies are eager to hire. The challenge isn't whether you have the right skills. The challenge is learning how to recognize them, refine them, and speak about them in a way that resonates with hiring managers.

Your journey on the field has already prepared you for what's next. You've learned how to stay motivated, adjust to challenges, and pursue excellence. Now, it's time to recognize those strengths for what they are, your competitive advantage, and use them to position yourself as a high-impact professional who's ready to win in any arena.

THE SKILLS CORPORATE LEADERS WANT AND HOW ATHLETES ALREADY HAVE THEM

DISCIPLINE: THE ABILITY TO STAY FOCUSED AND EXECUTE

Business leaders value people who can stay focused, follow through on their commitments, and consistently deliver results. You've already built that kind of discipline. It came from the structured routines, the early mornings, the long hours of training, and your commitment to goals that required daily effort—no shortcuts, no excuses.

That same dedication transfers directly into the workplace. In business, just like in sport, success doesn't come from occasional bursts of effort. It comes from showing up with consistency, staying locked in, and executing when it matters most. Discipline is what sets high performers apart, and you've already proven you have it.

Why This Matters:

In the corporate world, distractions, setbacks, and challenges occur. Those who maintain focus, execute plans, and maintain consistency are the ones who rise to the top.

How It Translates to Business:

- ✔ Staying committed to long-term projects despite setbacks.
- ✔ Keeping focused on the details that lead to big wins.
- ✔ Meeting deadlines and maintaining high performance without constant supervision.

TIME MANAGEMENT: PRIORITIZING AND EXECUTING EFFICIENTLY

Companies rely on people who can manage their workload, prioritize what matters most, and consistently meet deadlines. You've already done that every season, every semester, every day you balanced training, classes, recovery, and life. That wasn't just a schedule. That was time management at a high level.

Through sport, you learned how to stay organized, how to focus on the right things at the right time, and how to get things done under pressure. Those same skills are exactly what help professionals stay productive and effective in fast-paced environments. You've been managing your time like a pro for years. Now it's time to use that ability to thrive in your career.

Why This Matters:

Efficiency is crucial in the corporate world. Businesses want individuals who can maximize their productivity and focus on high-impact activities.

How It Translates to Business:

- ✔ Managing multiple projects and deadlines without feeling overwhelmed.
- ✔ Prioritizing tasks and focusing on high-impact activities.
- ✔ Staying productive and efficient in fast-paced environments.

STRATEGIC THINKING: MAKING QUICK AND EFFECTIVE DECISIONS

Business leaders count on people who can analyze situations, adapt quickly, and make smart decisions under pressure. You've been doing that your entire athletic career. Whether you were reading a defense, adjusting to an opponent's strategy, or making a fast call in the heat of the moment, you were building your ability to think strategically.

That skill doesn't stay on the field. It translates directly into the business world, where things move fast and the stakes are high. You know how to stay sharp, assess your options, and choose the right move under pressure. That mindset is a powerful asset in any career.

Why This Matters:

Strategic thinkers help businesses navigate uncertainty and seize opportunities. They analyze data quickly and make informed choices under pressure.

How It Translates to Business:

- ✔ Making data-driven and calculated decisions.
- ✔ Adapting quickly to changes in the market.
- ✔ Balancing risk and opportunity for maximum impact.

COMMUNICATION: EXPRESSING IDEAS CLEARLY AND EFFECTIVELY

You've had to communicate clearly with teammates, coaches, maybe even the media. You've learned how to speak up, listen actively, and adjust your message to the moment. That's not just good communication in sport. That's preparation for success in business.

In the corporate world, the ability to express your ideas clearly whether in writing, conversation, or even through body language is essential. Strong communicators build trust, prevent misunderstandings, and move teams forward. You already know how to communicate under pressure. Now it's about using that skill to make an even bigger impact in your career.

Why This Matters:

In business, miscommunication can lead to costly errors, delays, and missed opportunities. Clear communication ensures alignment, builds trusts, and drives productivity. Professionals who can articulate their thoughts confidently and listen actively increase their impact.

How It Translates to Business:

- ✔ Providing and receiving feedback constructively to strengthen collaboration.
- ✔ Adapting communication styles to suit different audiences (e.g. clients, colleagues, executives)
- ✔ Effectively listening, asking clarifying questions, and responding thoughtfully in meetings.

LEADERSHIP: INSPIRING AND ELEVATING OTHERS

Organizations thrive when people step up, take initiative, and inspire those around them to do their best work. That's leadership, and you've already lived it. Whether you wore the title of captain or led by example through your actions, you've guided others toward a common goal.

You've made tough decisions under pressure. You've communicated with clarity and purpose. You've helped your teammates stay focused through setbacks and stay motivated through the grind. That's what real leadership looks like. And now, those same instincts and experiences can help you lead in the workplace, no matter your role or title.

Why This Matters:

Businesses need leaders at every level. Even if you are not in a managerial position, your ability to step up, communicate effectively, and drive a team toward success makes you an irreplaceable asset.

How It Translates to Business:

- ✔ Managing and inspiring teams to perform at their best.
- ✔ Leading by example by setting high standards and work ethics.
- ✔ Navigating conflicts and bringing people together to achieve success.

TEAMWORK: COLLABORATION TOWARD A COMMON GOAL

Companies succeed when people collaborate, share responsibility, and stay focused on a common goal. You already know how powerful teamwork can be. You've lived it through practices, road trips, hard losses, and big wins. You've learned that success doesn't happen alone. It takes trust, communication, and the ability to play your role while supporting others in theirs.

You've seen how individual strengths come together to create something greater than the sum of its parts. That same approach applies in business. Whether you're working across departments or within a team, your ability to collaborate, adapt, and contribute makes you an essential part of any organization's success.

Why This Matters:

Companies do not succeed in silos. The best businesses are built on strong teams that understand collaboration, interdependence, and shared victories.

How It Translates to Business:

- ✔ Working effectively with colleagues from diverse backgrounds.
- ✔ Understanding roles within a team and maximizing individual strengths.
- ✔ Communicating and problem-solving as a unit to achieve common goals.

EMOTIONAL INTELLIGENCE: HANDLING PRESSURE AND BUILDING RELATIONSHIPS

Businesses need people who can navigate workplace dynamics, communicate with clarity, and manage emotions under pressure. You've already learned how to do that. Through the highs and lows of competition, you've stayed composed, responded with intention, and built strong relationships with the people around you.

Emotional intelligence is more than staying calm, it's about knowing yourself, reading the room, and choosing how to respond. In the workplace, those same skills help you manage stress, connect with others, and lead with empathy. You've practiced emotional control in some of the toughest moments sport can offer. Now, you can bring that strength into every professional environment you step into.

Why This Matters:

Workplaces function best when employees understand how to manage their emotions and relationships effectively. Self-awareness and empathy help individuals recognize their impact on others and adapt their behavior for more effective interactions.

How It Translates to Business:

- ✔ Building strong professional relationships and fostering teamwork.
- ✔ Managing stress and staying composed in high-pressure situations.
- ✔ Understanding and responding to colleagues' emotions to create a positive work environment.

COMPETITIVE DRIVE & WORK ETHIC: GOING THE EXTRA MILE

Companies want people who are driven to deliver results and go beyond what's expected. That's already how you operate. You've never been satisfied with just showing up. You've pushed to improve, challenged yourself daily, and competed not just against others but against your own potential.

You know that success doesn't come from talent alone. It takes relentless effort, focus, and the willingness to go the extra mile even when no one's watching. That mindset is gold in the business world. Your work ethic, your drive to win, and your refusal to settle for average are exactly what make you stand out on any team, in any industry.

Why This Matters:

Competitive employees bring energy, ambition, commitment, and a results-driven mentality to their organizations. When a company wants an edge over the competition, it needs people who bring that mindset to their work.

How It Translates to Business:

- ✔ Being dedicated to setting and surpassing performance targets.
- ✔ Taking initiative to exceed expectations and contribute to company success.
- ✔ Maintaining motivation, staying committed to goals, and persevering in challenging situations.

ADAPTABILITY & COACHABILITY: THE WILLINGNESS TO LEARN AND IMPROVE

In today's fast-changing business world, companies are looking for people who stay open, learn quickly, and keep getting better. That's how you've always grown. As an athlete, you listened to feedback, made adjustments, and stayed flexible when circumstances changed. You didn't just take criticism, you used it to improve.

That mindset is a competitive edge in the workplace. When you stay adaptable and coachable, you keep evolving. You're able to take on new challenges, shift when plans change, and grow into bigger roles. You've already proven that you're willing to learn and eager to improve. Now, that same approach will help you level up in your career.

Why This Matters:

In a constantly evolving business landscape, those who can quickly learn and adapt to changes will always stay ahead.

How It Translates to Business:

- ✔ Embracing change and innovation in the workplace.
- ✔ Accepting and applying feedback for professional growth.
- ✔ Continuously improving performance and productivity.

RESILIENCE: THRIVING UNDER PRESSURE AND OVERCOMING ADVERSITY

Business moves fast, and challenges are constant. Companies need people who can handle pressure, adapt to setbacks, and keep pushing forward. You've already trained for that. Through the grind of practice, the sting of losses, and the climb back from injuries, you built resilience. You learned how to stay focused when things got hard and how to bounce back even stronger.

That kind of mental toughness is a game-changer in the corporate world. When things don't go according to plan, and they often won't, you know how to respond. You don't fold under pressure. You stay in it, adjust, and keep moving forward. That ability to recover, refocus, and rise is what makes you a true asset in any environment.

Why This Matters:

In an unpredictable corporate environment, those who can recover quickly from failure and stay focused on the goal become invaluable assets. Resilience fuels innovation and keeps teams moving forward despite inevitable setbacks.

How It Translates to Business:

- ✔ Handling high-stakes projects and deadlines with confidence.

✔ Learning from mistakes and using
them as growth opportunities.

✔ Bouncing back from rejection or failure, whether in
sales, negotiations, or career progression.

📋 Practice Plan

You may not realize it yet, but every practice, every game, and every tough season has already prepared you for the professional world. Before you turn the page, take a step back. Your athletic career has already given you more than you might recognize. Habits, instincts, and ways of thinking that will carry over into every part of your professional life. You have trained your body, sharpened your mindset, and learned how to perform under pressure. But have you ever paused to consider what all of that means outside of sport?

This practice plan is your chance to start seeing the bigger picture. Not just who you were as an athlete, but who you are becoming. Use the **Career Playbook** section at the back of the book to record your reflections for each Practice Plan. It is a space to turn your athletic experiences into stories, examples, and insights you can use when building your resume or preparing for interviews. You will find opportunities like this throughout the book. Each one is designed to help you connect what you have learned in sport to who you are becoming as a professional. Begin by writing down three to five moments from your athletic experience that challenged you, changed you, or taught you something important. Do not overthink it. Just trust your gut and focus on what stands out.

Ask yourself:

→ What moments in my athletic journey made me proud, uncomfortable, or better?

→ When did I feel stretched, tested, or transformed?

→ What habits or ways of thinking stuck with me— even off the field?

→ How did being an athlete shape the way I respond to challenge or opportunity?

You do not need perfect answers. You do not need to turn this into a story just yet. Just start noticing the patterns. The choices you made. The experiences that shaped how you show up in the world. This is your foundation. By doing this exercise, you are not just reflecting on your sports journey. You are quietly preparing for your future interviews. You are building a personal bank of stories that will allow you to speak confidently about your strengths in a way that resonates with employers.

This is the beginning of your shift. From athlete to professional. From player to leader. From resume to real impact. The rest of the book will help you build from here. But first, give yourself the chance to recognize just how much you have already done and how much of it is still with you.

Grab a pen or open a new document and start writing.

▦ Postgame Recap

The transition from athletics to business is not a leap. It is a natural progression. Your training ground has prepared you well. Now it is time to take the skills you have mastered and use them to dominate your next arena: the professional world.

The strengths you developed through sport are exactly what employers are looking for. Your ability to perform under pressure, work as part of a team, and pursue goals with relentless focus makes you a valuable asset in any workplace. By recognizing your own potential, you can confidently step into roles where you will thrive and lead.

You have already proven you can perform under immense pressure, push past limitations, and commit to the pursuit of excellence. Now it is time to recognize your own value, seize the opportunities ahead, and step confidently into the corporate world with the same drive and determination that defined your athletic career.

3

DISCIPLINE

STRUCTURE THAT LEADS TO SUCCESS

BEHIND THE BENCH

I met Jamie when they were in college and when they were still finding their footing on the basketball court. The talent was obvious, but the performance was unpredictable. That changed the night they missed a key shot and we lost a close game. Something shifted after that. Jamie built a routine: early gym sessions, stat tracking, film study. They trained like every rep mattered. We kept focused on something no one had told them before: practice doesn't make perfect—*perfect* practice makes perfect.

Years later, Jamie wasn't on the court. They were leading a team at a fast-growing logistics company. But their habits hadn't changed. They structured their days like practice: focused, goal-oriented, executed with discipline. Meetings ran like huddles. Deadlines were game-time. And when pressure hit, Jamie was steady. They had already rehearsed that moment a hundred different ways. Basketball didn't just make Jamie a better athlete. It made them a disciplined leader, someone who could build systems, stay accountable, and guide others through high-stakes moments with calm, practiced precision.

THE ROLE OF DISCIPLINE IN ATHLETIC SUCCESS

Discipline in sports is nonnegotiable. From a young age, you learn that natural talent will only take you so far. True greatness comes from consistency, repetition, and hard work. Whether it means sticking to a demanding training schedule, refining your technique through endless drills, or making difficult lifestyle choices to support your performance, discipline is what separates those who merely participate from those who rise to the top.

Athletes understand:

→ **Effort must be sustained.** Success is not about short bursts of motivation but about showing up every day and putting in the work.

→ **Sacrifices lead to long-term gains.** Waking up early, maintaining proper nutrition, and skipping social events are necessary to reach peak performance.

→ **Every detail matters.** Each practice, repetition, and play contributes to overall improvement and excellence.

→ **Consistency builds trust.** Just as reliability strengthens a team, it also establishes credibility in professional and personal relationships.

→ **Focus and preparation drive success.** Long-term achievement comes from disciplined preparation, even when faced with short-term obstacles.

This level of discipline is not just about physical training. It also shapes your mental toughness, emotional control, and ability to stay focused when the pressure is high. These are the attributes that make you valuable in the corporate world. You have already practiced staying composed, showing up with purpose, and doing what needs to be done, even when it is difficult. That kind of consistency and self-control is exactly what sets you apart in any professional environment.

HOW DISCIPLINE TRANSLATES TO BUSINESS SUCCESS

Being an athlete taught me to deal with pressure, to prepare better than anyone else, and to never expect overnight success.

— *Maria Sharapova*

It's easy to look at Maria Sharapova and see only the highlight reel: five Grand Slam titles, a world number 1 ranking, and international fame. But if you asked her what really made the difference, it wasn't talent or trophies, it was discipline. The kind of discipline forged not in front of cameras, but in the silent hours of early mornings and late-night recoveries, in the grind of training when no one was watching.

That mindset didn't end with her tennis career. Sharapova launched Sugarpova, a candy company she built from the ground up. What many assumed was a celebrity-branded product was, in fact, a serious business venture. She funded it herself, obsessing over details—from flavor to font. She read retail contracts like game tape and approached distribution strategy the same way she'd prepare for a Grand Slam opponent: systematically and with intent.

The transition looked smooth from the outside, but what powered it was the same thing that had carried her through years on tour: structured routines, long-term vision, and an almost stubborn commitment to doing the work every single day. In many ways, Sharapova never stopped competing. She just changed the playing field. And what she proved is that discipline isn't just what drives greatness in sport. It's what builds staying power, everywhere.

WHY DISCIPLINE IS A KEY DIFFERENTIATOR IN THE WORKPLACE

Many professionals struggle with discipline, especially in environments where distractions are constant, deadlines shift, and accountability is unclear. This is where you stand out. Your ability to stay committed, push through discomfort, and maintain high standards makes you an asset in any professional setting. Your background as an athlete reflects years of training in responsibility, consistency, and perseverance.

Employers appreciate individuals who:

→ Commit to long term goals and show up every day ready to perform

→ Stay focused and reliable under pressure

→ Hold themselves accountable and maintain high personal standards

→ Push through challenges without losing momentum or motivation

You bring a level of discipline that cannot be taught overnight. You are used to operating under pressure, bouncing back from setbacks, and doing the hard work even when no one is watching. This discipline forms the foundation for strong leadership. You set the bar high, lead by example, and understand that consistent effort and accountability are what drive lasting success.

THE PSYCHOLOGICAL BENEFITS OF DISCIPLINE

Beyond career success, discipline brings powerful psychological benefits. It strengthens your resilience, builds emotional stability, and reinforces a strong sense of self confidence. When you master discipline, you learn how to manage stress, regulate your emotions, and develop a mindset that focuses on growth. These are the qualities that help you handle setbacks, stay focused, and keep striving for excellence no matter the challenge.

The mental fortitude developed through disciplined habits helps individuals have:

→ **Sustained motivation**—Discipline fosters perseverance, allowing individuals to stay committed to their goals despite failures or obstacles.

→ **Emotional control**—Practicing discipline helps individuals regulate their emotions, maintaining composure even in high-pressure situations.

→ **Stronger self-confidence**—Consistently following through on commitments builds trust in one's abilities and reinforces self-belief.

→ **Enhanced decision-making**—Disciplined individuals develop the ability to make sound choices, even when faced with stress or uncertainty.

→ **Long-term vision**—A disciplined mindset prioritizes growth and long-term success over short-term comfort or gratification.

BUILDING A CULTURE OF DISCIPLINE IN THE WORKPLACE

You have seen firsthand what discipline can do for a team. You know how it sets the tone, raises expectations, and builds trust. Now, as you transition into the professional world, you have the opportunity to bring that same mindset into your next environment and help build a culture of discipline wherever you go.

It starts with how you show up. When you hold yourself accountable, follow through on commitments, and stay focused on your goals, people notice. When you bring consistency, structure, and a drive for excellence, you set the standard for others. That is how a culture begins. One person modeling what it means to be dependable, prepared, and growth minded.

You are not just stepping into a company. You are stepping into a new team. The same way you once helped shape the identity of your athletic program, you now have the chance to shape the identity of your workplace. Culture is built from the inside out, and your discipline is one of the strongest tools you bring to the table.

CORPORATE APPLICATION OF DISCIPLINE
Meeting Deadlines and Delivering Quality Work on Time

You are used to strict schedules and high expectations. In sports, missing a deadline—whether it was a conditioning target, a game plan, or a critical strategy — could be the difference between winning and losing. That same urgency carries into the business world. Punctuality and reliability are not just appreciated, they are essential. They build your credibility, keep things moving forward, and show that you can be trusted to deliver when it matters most.

How athletes apply this:

- ✔ Managing multiple responsibilities without missing key deadlines.

- ✔ Balancing workload efficiently, just as they balance training and academics.

- ✔ Delivering high-quality work, even under time constraints.

- ✔ Understanding the importance of preparation and execution under pressure.

- ✔ Prioritizing tasks to optimize productivity and maintain effectiveness.

Staying Committed to Professional Growth and Skill Development

You do not just show up. You work to improve every single day. You review film, analyze mistakes, and train with intention. That same mindset applies to your career. Professionals who grow are the ones who take ownership of their development, stay focused on progress, and keep sharpening their skills to stay ahead. You already know how to do this. Now it is about applying that same level of purpose to your growth off the field.

How athletes apply this:

- ✔ Seeking continuous learning opportunities, such as certifications or mentorships.

✔ Accepting feedback constructively and making necessary adjustments.

✔ Setting long-term career goals and breaking them down into actionable steps.

✔ Demonstrating resilience and a willingness to adapt when faced with challenges.

✔ Taking initiative to expand knowledge, just as athletes refine their techniques.

Demonstrating Reliability and Consistency in the Workplace

In sports, your teammates and coaches counted on you to show up and perform, no matter how you felt that day. That same dependability is just as important in the workplace. Your ability to follow through on commitments and deliver consistent results builds trust. When others know they can count on you, you become a steady force on any team, and that kind of reliability sets you apart.

How athletes apply this:

✔ Arriving prepared and ready to contribute every day, much like they would for practice or competition.

✔ Holding themselves accountable for their work, just as they would for their athletic performance.

✔ Maintaining focus and effort, even when tasks become routine or challenging.

- ✓ Understanding that consistency builds leadership credibility and team trust.

- ✓ Remaining composed and focused under high-stakes situations.

📋 Practice Plan—Structure that Leads to Success

Discipline isn't about being perfect—it's about being consistent. It's showing up and executing with purpose, even when it's inconvenient, uncomfortable, or unexciting. As an athlete, you lived this every day. Now, it's time to see where that mindset fits in your career. This exercise will help you identify how your discipline has shaped your habits and how those habits can fuel your professional life. You're not starting from scratch. You're just learning to apply the same mindset in a new arena.

→ Identify one routine from your athletic life that required daily discipline. (Examples: early lifts, conditioning, film review, injury rehab, nutrition tracking)

→ Describe how you stayed consistent, especially on the days when it would've been easier not to. What pushed you to keep going? What strategies or mental habits helped you follow through?

→ Now map that routine to a business context. If you could bring that same discipline into your professional life, where would it make a difference? Meeting deadlines? Preparing for presentations or projects? Sticking to a development goal?

➜ Write a simple daily or weekly "discipline rep" you can commit to now. This should be small, repeatable, and structured. (Examples: review your schedule every morning, block one hour daily for focused work, prep for meetings the night before, set weekly learning goals.)

By turning discipline into a daily habit, not just a memory from sport, you're building the foundation for sustained success in your career. You already know how to train with structure.

Now you're using that same muscle to grow as a professional. Grab a pen and run the drill.

Postgame Recap

Discipline is the foundation that supports both athletic and professional success. As a student athlete, the habits you built on the field, like early mornings, extra reps, and deep commitment, are the same habits that will help you excel in your career. You already have what it takes to thrive in the business world. The key is recognizing the value of your discipline, shaping it to fit a new environment, and bringing the same level of focus and drive that once powered your athletic journey. When you do that, your results will speak for themselves.

4

TIME MANAGEMENT

BALANCING MULTIPLE RESPONSIBILITIES

BEHIND THE BENCH

When I first worked with Jamie, discipline was their breakthrough. After blowing a late-game rotation and sitting with the weight of it, they committed to the daily grind of early gym sessions, film study, no excuses. It changed the trajectory of their game. But what tested them even more wasn't the court. It was the calendar.

They thought they understood busy, until they had to plan their entire life around the team schedule and the additional training they added to improve their performance. Morning lifts at 6:00 a.m. Class from 8:00 to 2:00. Film review squeezed in over lunch. Practice by 3:30. Training room. Homework.

Study hall. Team meetings. Travel days that stole weekends. Somewhere in there, they had to sleep, eat, and still show up to class as if they hadn't just run stairs for 45 minutes at dawn.

There was no margin for error. One missed assignment, one forgotten drill, and it snowballed into academic penalties, bench time, tension with coaches. For the first month, Jamie lived in constant reaction mode: rushing from place to place, cutting corners, surviving.

But then something shifted. Jamie realized they couldn't just *work harder*. They had to manage smarter. They started building systems. A calendar that mapped out every hour of the day, including breaks. Weekly check-ins with their academic advisor. Packing bags the night before road games. Setting reminders for hydration, meals, recovery. They learned how to prioritize what *had* to happen versus what could flex. Time became a series of intentional choices, not just a blur of commitments. It didn't just improve their grades or stats. It gave them room to breathe mentally, physically, emotionally. They weren't less busy. They were just better aligned.

Years later, that same skillset of scheduling with intention, planning backward from outcomes, and knowing when to say no became their advantage in business. Meetings, deadlines, family, leadership responsibilities, it all worked better because they had lived through a schedule where every minute mattered.

Jamie didn't just learn to manage time in college. They learned to *own it*. And it started with a color-coded calendar, a pair of basketball shoes, and the realization that high performance requires more than effort. It requires structure.

THE ROLE OF TIME MANAGEMENT IN ATHLETIC SUCCESS

Student athletes are masters of time management. Between academics, training, games, and personal commitments, you have constantly balanced multiple responsibilities. The demands of being a student athlete have required efficiency, discipline, and a strategic approach to managing time. Your ability to juggle these tasks without missing deadlines, sacrificing performance, or compromising your well-being is a skill that translates directly into the professional world.

In business, deadlines, meetings, and projects often overlap. That makes time management an essential part of success. Just like in sports, professionals must prioritize tasks, stay organized, and maintain a high level of productivity across competing demands.

As a former athlete, your experience balancing athletic and academic responsibilities is a powerful asset. You understand the value of time, and you have already developed systems for managing it effectively. In the workplace, this becomes a key differentiator. Being able to handle complex schedules, meet tight deadlines, and deliver high quality results makes you someone employers can count on.

In sports, time management is not optional. Your schedule was packed with training, travel, competitions, and responsibilities off the field. You learned early that success does not come from just working harder, but from working smarter and more efficiently. You know how to avoid distractions, stay focused, and make every moment count.

Athletes understand:

→ **Every minute counts.** With so many responsibilities, time must be used effectively to make room for training, rest, and other commitments.

→ **Prioritization is key.** Whether it's deciding which assignment to tackle first or when to rest and recover, athletes understand the importance of making strategic decisions about where to allocate their time.

→ **Deadlines are a reality.** Whether it's a game day, a project deadline, or a test, athletes are accustomed to working under tight timelines and performing when it matters most.

→ **Focus and discipline matter.** By committing to a structured schedule, athletes can manage their time in ways that lead to peak performance across multiple areas of their lives.

→ **Flexibility is important.** Even with a set schedule, athletes know how to adapt to unforeseen circumstances, like a change in practice times or a last-minute game. This flexibility is vital in managing time effectively, especially when unexpected challenges arise.

These habits and skills translate directly into the business world, where juggling multiple tasks and priorities is a daily occurrence.

HOW TIME MANAGEMENT TRANSLATES TO BUSINESS SUCCESS

"Being a student-athlete has taught me how to organize my life, prioritize what matters, and still perform under pressure."

— Myron Rolle

It's easy to talk about grit and balance in theory. But Myron Rolle lived it. While playing football at Florida State University, Rolle wasn't just a standout safety, but he was also a pre-med student with a 3.75 GPA and a Rhodes Scholar, one of the most prestigious academic honors in the world. At a time when most NCAA athletes were trying to balance early lifts, classes, and practice, Rolle was squeezing in neuroscience labs, MCAT prep, and international scholarship interviews. He wasn't juggling. He was strategizing.

His days were tightly structured. Early mornings meant film study and conditioning. Midday was packed with classes and lab work. Evenings were for practice. Late nights were for textbooks, not downtime. Every hour had a purpose. When he earned the Rhodes Scholarship and took a year off football to study at Oxford, some questioned whether he'd be ready for the NFL. He was. He later played for the Tennessee Titans before pursuing his real dream: medicine.

Today, Myron Rolle is a neurosurgeon. He credits his success not just to intelligence or talent, but to the time management habits he forged during his years as a student-athlete. Discipline, structure, and clarity. He learned to say no, to plan ahead, to build in rest without wasting time. Football gave him intensity. Medicine required endurance. His habits, built in the crucible of NCAA pressure, gave him both.

Myron Rolle's story is a reminder that the real challenge isn't doing one thing well, it's learning how to do many things without letting any of them drop. And that's not a gift. It's a practiced skill.

WHY TIME MANAGEMENT IS A KEY DIFFERENTIATOR IN THE WORKPLACE

In the corporate world, time management can be the difference between success and failure. Companies value employees who can juggle multiple priorities without sacrificing quality or efficiency. As a former athlete, you have already honed the ability to manage demanding schedules. You are naturally equipped to excel in environments where time is a limited resource. Your experience balancing academics, athletics, and personal responsibilities allows you to navigate business challenges with confidence and clarity.

Employers appreciate individuals who:

→ Consistently meet deadlines and deliver results on time.

→ Manage competing demands effectively, focusing on the highest priorities.

→ Stay organized and productive under pressure.

→ Take a proactive approach to their workload, using time intentionally rather than letting tasks pile up.

You bring a high level of time management expertise that allows you to perform at your best, no matter how demanding your schedule becomes. Your ability to handle multiple projects, stay on track, and deliver strong results is a powerful advantage. It sets you apart in the workplace and shows that you are ready to lead in any environment.

THE PSYCHOLOGICAL BENEFITS OF TIME MANAGEMENT

Beyond professional success, time management has profound psychological benefits. It fosters a sense of control, reduces stress, and enhances mental clarity. When you manage your time effectively, you experience greater confidence, improved focus, and a stronger sense of accomplishment. These are the qualities that support both your well-being and your ability to stay productive in high-pressure environments.

The mental clarity and emotional balance gained through strong time management help you:

→ **Reduced stress**—Planning ahead and staying organized helps you avoid last minute pressure and missed deadlines.

→ **Greater sense of control**—Managing your schedule with intention, rather than reaction, allows you to feel more in command of your time.

→ **Increased job satisfaction**—Completing tasks on schedule fosters a sense of achievement and fulfillment in your work.

YOUR COMPETITIVE ADVANTAGE

→ **Improved focus and mental clarity**—Minimizing distractions and structuring your time enables deeper concentration on important tasks.

→ **Boosted confidence and motivation**—Successfully managing your time reinforces self belief and fuels continued productivity.

These habits do more than help you succeed at work. They shape a mindset of calm, control, and clarity that will serve you well wherever your journey takes you.

BUILDING A CULTURE OF TIME MANAGEMENT IN THE WORKPLACE

You already know what it means to manage your time with precision. As an athlete, your success depended on how well you organized your day, prioritized your efforts, and stayed on track. That skill does not disappear when you step away from the game. It becomes one of your greatest assets in the professional world. Time management is not just about staying busy. It is about staying effective, and you have already mastered that balance under pressure.

When you bring that mindset into the workplace, you do more than manage your own time well. You help shape the environment around you. By modeling discipline, structure, and proactive planning, you become a quiet leader. Your ability to stay on task, meet expectations, and deliver results builds trust. It helps teammates stay

44

focused, projects stay on track, and goals get met without last minute scrambles.

You can influence workplace culture simply by being consistent. When others see how you organize your time, communicate about priorities, and respond to pressure with clarity instead of chaos, they learn from you. You may not hold a formal leadership title, but your habits speak loudly. You show others what it looks like to take ownership of your day and make every minute count.

Your time management skills are more than just helpful. They are contagious. And when you use them well, you do not just perform. You lead.

CORPORATE APPLICATION OF TIME MANAGEMENT
Prioritizing Tasks and Meeting Tight Deadlines

In the corporate world, deadlines often overlap and priorities shift quickly. Being able to prioritize tasks based on urgency, importance, and available resources is essential to ensuring that the most critical projects are completed on time. As an athlete, you have already trained yourself to navigate this kind of pressure. You know what it means to prepare for a big game while still managing schoolwork, recovery, and team responsibilities. That same experience now gives you an edge in fast-moving professional environments. You have learned how to stay focused, make smart choices with your time, and deliver when it matters most. Those instincts are not just helpful, they are powerful tools for driving results in any job you take on.

How athletes apply this:

- ✔ Assessing the urgency and importance of tasks to ensure deadlines are met without sacrificing quality.

- ✔ Breaking large tasks into smaller, manageable steps and setting realistic deadlines for each.

- ✔ Managing time effectively in high-pressure situations, just as they would before a big game or competition.

- ✔ Learning how to quickly pivot priorities when unexpected demands or changes arise, like a last-minute meeting or urgent project request.

Balancing Multiple Projects Without Compromising Quality

You already know how to divide your attention between competing demands. Whether it was balancing training sessions with academic work or preparing for back-to-back competitions, you learned how to manage your time without letting any part of your performance suffer. That ability to stay sharp across multiple priorities is one of your greatest strengths. In business, professionals are expected to manage several projects at once, often under pressure. Your experience has already trained you to handle that kind of complexity. You know how to stay focused, keep quality high, and deliver results even when your plate is full. That is what makes you stand out.

How athletes apply this:

- ✔ Creating a schedule that allows enough time for each task while still maintaining focus on quality and performance.

- ✔ Avoiding the temptation to procrastinate by staying proactive and tackling each project with full attention.

- ✔ Learning how to delegate tasks when necessary and collaborate with others to ensure high-quality outcomes.

- ✔ Staying focused on the task at hand, even when juggling multiple responsibilities, by managing time effectively.

Maximizing Productivity by Staying Organized and Proactive

Organization is the foundation of effective time management. As an athlete, you learned to structure your days with intention, planning your training, tracking your nutrition, and building in recovery to stay at your best. That same mindset applies directly to your professional life. When you stay organized, you are not just keeping things in order, you are setting yourself up to perform at a high level. In business, organization allows you to manage your workload efficiently, reduce unnecessary stress, and focus your energy on what matters most. Time management is not only about finding space in your schedule, it is about making every minute count.

How athletes apply this:

- ✔ Using tools like calendars, planners, and to-do lists to stay on top of commitments and deadlines.

- ✔ Preparing in advance for meetings, projects, or upcoming events, just as they would prepare for a game or practice session.

- ✔ Keeping track of long-term goals while maintaining focus on short-term tasks, ensuring a balanced and productive approach to work.

- ✔ Being proactive in addressing potential obstacles or delays, rather than reacting after they occur.

📋 Practice Plan

As an athlete, you did not just show up and hope things worked out. You planned. You managed your schedule with intention, making time for practices, lifts, games, travel, school, and recovery. You had systems, checklists, and routines that helped you stay on track and perform consistently. Whether you realized it or not, you were already practicing the kind of time management that professionals work hard to develop.

Now it is time to recognize that skill and learn how to carry it forward. In this exercise, reflect on how you have used structure and organization to stay productive in your athletic life. Write out your responses to the following prompts:

→ Think of a time when your schedule was packed with training, class, meetings, travel, and more. How did you stay organized? What tools did you use, such as a planner, whiteboard, or calendar app?

→ What habits helped you stay one step ahead, like packing your bag the night before, reviewing your weekly schedule, or prepping your meals in advance?

→ How did you keep your short-term tasks aligned with long-term goals, like season performance, academic success, or personal development?

→ When did being proactive make the difference, such as catching a potential conflict or avoiding a last minute scramble?

→ How did being organized help reduce your stress, improve your performance, or earn trust from others?

Now, look at your current or upcoming professional life. Time management is not just about being busy. It is about being ready. The same way you approached game day with a plan, you can approach your career with a structure that keeps you focused and in control. Where could you apply these same strategies to meetings, assignments, or long term projects? What habits or tools already work for you, and what could you improve?

Write down one organizational tool or time management routine from your athletic life that you want to carry into your next chapter. Then write one new habit you would like to experiment with now, whether it is setting a weekly planning

YOUR COMPETITIVE ADVANTAGE

session, using a calendar more consistently, or prepping each day the night before.

Grab a pen or open a new page and start building your system.

Postgame Recap

Time management is a vital skill for both athletic and business success. As a student-athlete, your ability to balance academics, training, and personal commitments became a training ground for the demands of the corporate world. Your experience managing tight schedules, meeting deadlines, and maximizing productivity gives you a real advantage in the workplace. These are not just habits you picked up—they are high-performance strategies. The key to success is not just working hard, but working smart. When you apply the time management techniques you developed in sports to your professional life, you set yourself apart. You are prepared to thrive, lead, and succeed in any environment where time is a valuable resource.

5

STRATEGIC THINKING

MAKING QUICK AND EFFECTIVE DECISIONS

BEHIND THE BENCH

By Jamie's third year, the fundamentals were locked in. They had the discipline. They had the systems. They could manage the schedule, juggle responsibilities, and show up prepared. But the next evolution wasn't about structure. It was about speed. How quickly could they process, decide, and act.

I remember one game in particular. Tight score, under a minute left, and Jamie had the ball on the wing. The play that was drawn up wasn't there. The defense over-rotated. For a second—just a second—they hesitated. And then, in real time, Jamie made a completely different read. Skip pass to the corner. Open three. Game.

What impressed me wasn't just that it worked. It was *how* Jamie made the decision. Calm. Clear. Immediate. Not reactive, but strategic. That kind of choice doesn't come from instinct alone. It comes from preparation, pattern recognition, and trust in yourself and in the system you've built. That season, I started to see it everywhere. Jamie wasn't just playing harder, they were thinking sharper. On the court, they saw mismatches a step ahead. Off the court, they were taking control in film sessions, offering reads, suggesting counters, adjusting mid-practice without being prompted. The game slowed down for them, and their mind moved faster. What Jamie had developed was more than confidence. It was strategic thinking. The ability to stay composed in motion. To weigh options quickly. To trust the process without becoming rigid. To act, not react.

And later, in business, that same ability became their edge. Fast-changing markets, high-stakes meetings, last-minute pivots—Jamie could assess and decide without getting stuck. Not because they always had perfect information, but because they had built the habits of clarity, trust, and calm under pressure. They didn't wait for the perfect answer. They moved with purpose and adjusted on the fly. Quick thinking isn't about rushing. It's about *readiness*. And Jamie had trained for that moment long before it arrived.

THE ROLE OF STRATEGIC THINKING IN ATHLETIC SUCCESS

In the world of sports, success often hinges on your ability to make quick, strategic decisions under pressure. Whether it is reading a defense as a quarterback, anticipating your opponent's next move on the tennis court, or deciding whether to pass or take the shot in a basketball game, you are constantly analyzing and adapting. Your ability to assess situations rapidly, weigh risks, and act decisively is a hallmark of strategic thinking.

In business, you will rely on that same skill. You will face complex challenges, shifting priorities, and competitive environments that demand sharp decision-making. Strategic thinkers like you evaluate data, identify patterns, and make informed choices even when the clock is ticking. Your capacity to think critically, consider multiple variables, and adapt on the fly is a powerful advantage in today's fast-paced corporate world.

Strategic thinking is not just about solving problems. It is about identifying opportunities, mitigating risks, and creating the conditions for innovation and progress. Employers value professionals who can see the bigger picture, think ahead, and make calculated decisions that lead to long-term success.

Athletes understand:

→ **Split-second decisions matter.** The right call in a tight moment often made the difference between winning and losing. You relied on your instincts, your training, and your preparation.

→ **Adaptability is essential.** You knew no game ever went exactly as planned. You adjusted in real time and responded to changing conditions, evolving strategies, and unexpected challenges.

→ **Data informs decisions.** You studied game footage, tracked your performance, and learned from results. You used information to prepare smarter and perform better.

→ **Risk and reward are always in play.** You learned when to take a shot and when to play it safe. You weighed options and made decisions with purpose and intention.

→ **Mental agility is key.** You stayed calm in pressure-filled moments. You kept your focus and made smart choices even when everything was on the line.

You are already a strategic thinker. Now, it is about recognizing that skill, refining it for your next chapter, and bringing it forward with confidence. The mindset that helped you win in sport will help you lead, innovate, and succeed in business.

HOW STRATEGIC THINKING TRANSLATES TO BUSINESS SUCCESS

"You have to make decisions before the ball even gets to you. That's where the game is really played."

— *Megan Rapinoe*

Megan Rapinoe built her career on sharp thinking under pressure. On the soccer field, she was never the most physically dominant player—but she rarely needed to be. She saw the game seconds ahead. She knew where the space would be, what her teammates needed, and how to create openings with precision and timing. For Rapinoe, the real work happened before the ball even reached her feet.

That mindset didn't stay on the pitch. Off the field, Rapinoe has become a savvy, high-impact figure in the worlds of business, branding, and activism. She's launched and co-founded multiple ventures, from lifestyle brands to media platforms, and negotiated endorsement deals not just for visibility, but for *values*. She reads people and situations the same way she read defenders—quickly, intuitively, and with a game plan in mind.

Where other athletes sign endorsement deals, Rapinoe builds partnerships. She doesn't just ask, "What will this brand do for me?" but "What will we build together?" Her collaboration with Nike was about more than product—it was about storytelling, platform-building, and pushing forward conversations around equity. Her co-founding of the gender-neutral lifestyle brand *re—inc* with teammates was equally intentional: a play not for profit alone, but for purpose-driven business.

In negotiations, she uses the same skills that shaped her play: reading cues, understanding positioning, and timing her asks. She's not afraid to challenge, but she doesn't move without strategy. Whether sitting in a C-suite meeting or testifying before Congress, she speaks with clarity earned from years of high-pressure play, where stakes were high and mistakes were public.

The lesson Megan Rapinoe brings into every business room is the same one that defined her career: success doesn't come from reacting—it comes from anticipating. From preparing. From knowing your field better than anyone else. Whether it's a World Cup final or a boardroom full of executives, she shows up with the same focus. And just like on the pitch, when she moves, people pay attention.

WHY STRATEGIC THINKING IS A KEY DIFFERENTIATOR IN THE WORKPLACE

Strategic thinking is one of the most powerful skills you can bring to your career. In the corporate world, professionals who think critically, anticipate challenges, and make effective decisions stand out. Your ability to analyze complex situations, stay composed under pressure, and make sound, data-driven choices makes you an invaluable asset wherever you go.

When you apply your strategic mindset in the workplace, you bring strengths that companies rely on every day. You know how to:

→ Navigate uncertainty with confidence.
→ Make informed decisions based on data and preparation.
→ Identify opportunities for growth and innovation.
→ Adapt quickly to changes and shifting priorities.

As a former athlete, you already have an edge. You are used to making quick, calculated decisions when it counts. You understand how to read the situation, assess risk, adjust your strategy, and execute. That experience translates directly into your career. Strategic planning, situational awareness, and adaptability are your strengths. In a fast-moving business environment, those are the exact qualities that set you apart.

THE PSYCHOLOGICAL BENEFITS OF STRATEGIC THINKING

Beyond its practical applications, strategic thinking also gives you a mental edge. It helps you stay proactive, always looking for ways to improve, grow, and stay ahead of the game. When you approach challenges with a strategic mindset, you build resilience, sharpen your focus, and strengthen your ability to problem-solve. You stay calm under pressure because you are already thinking a few steps ahead.

Here are just a few of the psychological benefits you gain through strategic thinking:

→ **Stronger decision-making confidence**—You build trust in your judgment by looking at situations from different angles and making thoughtful choices.

→ **Improved problem-solving ability**—You use analytical thinking to break down challenges and find solutions that work.

→ **Greater adaptability**—You stay composed and flexible when things change, adjusting quickly to new obstacles or plans.

→ **Sharper focus and long-term vision**—You keep your attention on what truly matters and let go of distractions that pull you off course.

Strategic thinking is more than just a skill, it is a mindset that keeps you grounded, focused, and ready for whatever comes next. You have already developed it in sport. Now, you can use it to lead in business and in life.

BUILDING A CULTURE OF STRATEGIC THINKING IN THE WORKPLACE

Organizations that value strategic thinking foster cultures where innovation, adaptability, and forward momentum are the norm. As someone who has competed at a high level, you bring a mindset rooted in preparation, adaptability, and long-term thinking. These qualities can help shape a workplace culture that embraces critical analysis and welcomes new ideas.

Look for environments where questioning assumptions is encouraged, where team members are invited to think critically and challenge the status quo in constructive ways. Seek out organizations that invest in strategic development through mentorship, professional learning, and cross-functional collaboration. These opportunities will help you refine your ability to think several steps ahead and make sound decisions under pressure.

Great cultures also recognize innovative thinking and reward smart risk-taking. If bold ideas are welcomed and thoughtful experimentation is encouraged, your instincts and vision will be assets. Finally, look for a team that values data and evidence. Just as you used stats, film, and performance metrics to sharpen your game, you'll thrive in a workplace that makes decisions based on insight and feedback.

When you bring your strategic mindset into this kind of environment, you elevate those around you. You help create a culture that is more resilient, agile, and forward-thinking just like the teams you succeeded with in sport.

CORPORATE APPLICATION OF STRATEGIC THINKING:
Making Data-Driven and Calculated Decisions

As a strategic thinker, you know that relying on instincts alone isn't enough. You make your best decisions when you back them up with facts. Just like you studied game footage to spot patterns, adjust your technique, and improve your performance, you can bring that same approach to business. Whether you are reviewing performance metrics, analyzing trends, or digging into customer feedback, your ability to interpret data and apply it to your decision-making gives you a serious edge. You're not just reacting, you're leading with intention and insight.

How athletes apply this:

- ✔ Using performance statistics to identify strengths and weaknesses.

- ✔ Analyzing opponents' tendencies and adapting strategies accordingly.

- ✔ Using game analytics to make smarter, data-backed plays.

Adapting Quickly to Changes in the Market

Just like you had to adjust your game plan in response to your opponent's strategy, you'll need to pivot quickly in business when the market shifts, trends change, or unexpected challenges arise. Your ability to adapt in real time, stay focused, and make sharp decisions under pressure is one of your greatest assets, and it will serve you just as powerfully in your career as it did in competition.

How athletes apply this:

- ✔ Shifting tactics mid-game to counter opponents' strategies.
- ✔ Modifying training regimens based on new performance goals.
- ✔ Adapting to different playing conditions, such as weather or field changes.

Balancing Risk and Opportunity for Maximum Impact

You know that playing it safe does not always lead to victory. In your sport, you took calculated risks, whether it was going for the tough play, making an unexpected move, or trusting your instincts in a high stakes moment. Those risks often created your biggest breakthroughs. The same applies in business. Strategic thinkers like you weigh risks and rewards carefully, then make bold decisions that drive results. Your courage to take smart chances and your ability to evaluate outcomes gives you a powerful advantage in any competitive environment.

How athletes apply this:

- ✔ Taking bold shots or making aggressive plays when the payoff is worth the risk.

- ✔ Accepting calculated risks during competition to gain a competitive edge.

- ✔ Deciding when to push forward or hold back based on situational awareness.

Long-Term Vision and Goal-Oriented Thinking

You know that playing it safe does not always lead to victory. In your sport, you took calculated risks, whether it was going for the tough play, making an unexpected move, or trusting your instincts in a high stakes moment. Those decisions often led to your biggest breakthroughs. The same applies in business. Strategic thinkers like you weigh risks and rewards with care, then make bold moves that drive real results. Your willingness to take smart chances and your ability to evaluate outcomes give you a powerful edge in any competitive environment.

How athletes apply this:

- ✔ Setting long-term goals for performance improvement.

- ✔ Training consistently with future competitions in mind.

- ✔ Developing strategies for career longevity and peak performance.

📋 Practice Plan

Strategic thinking is all about seeing the big picture and making smart decisions under pressure. As an athlete, you have done this more often than you may realize. You adjusted your game plan on the fly, weighed risks in key moments, and stayed one step ahead of your opponent. This exercise will help you reflect on those moments and begin to understand how that same mindset can be applied in business.

Answer the following questions to explore how you've already used strategic thinking in your athletic experience:

→ When did I need to shift my tactics mid-game or mid-season? What changed, and how did I respond?

→ What's an example of a time I took a calculated risk in competition? What made me decide it was worth it?

→ How did I balance long-term goals with short-term decisions—whether in training, recovery, or performance?

→ When did I have to make a quick decision under pressure? What factors did I consider in the moment?

Now take a moment to consider: how can this same way of thinking apply in your professional life? How will you respond when a project shifts direction halfway through? What will you do when you're asked to make a decision with limited information and high stakes? Whether you're solving problems, leading a team, or navigating change, your ability to think strategically will set you apart.

Grab a pen—or open a new document—and start thinking it through.

Postgame Recap

Strategic thinking is a powerful skill that bridges the gap between your athletic excellence and future business success. Your ability to assess situations, adapt quickly, and make effective decisions is just as valuable in the boardroom as it was on the playing field. You have already learned how to stay composed under pressure, pivot when necessary, and make smart, timely choices that influence outcomes. That experience gives you a unique and valuable edge in the corporate world. With your strategic mindset, you are equipped to seize opportunities, overcome challenges, and create lasting impact in any career you choose.

6

COMMUNICATION

EXPRESSING IDEAS CLEARLY AND EFFECTIVELY

BEHIND THE BENCH

For a long time, Jamie led with actions, not words. They showed up early, outworked everyone, made smart decisions in tight moments—but when it came to speaking up, they held back. It wasn't fear. It was habit. Their mindset was: *do your job, let the work speak for itself.* That worked—for a while.

But by senior year, something shifted. Jamie wasn't just executing plays—they were seeing the game unfold, anticipating decisions, setting the tone in huddles. And eventually, people started looking to them not just for performance, but for clarity. For direction. For voice. I remember one team meeting before a road game that had playoff implications. The room was tense.

Coaches were talking, but it wasn't landing. Then Jamie spoke with a voice that was calm, focused, and brief. They laid out what needed to happen on the court, but more than that, they gave the team *language to lock into*. Something clicked. The energy shifted. And we played one of our most cohesive games all season.

That was the moment I saw it clearly: Jamie wasn't just communicating. They were connecting through communication. It wasn't about volume. It was about *precision*. Whether breaking down film, encouraging a teammate, or challenging the group in the locker room, Jamie had learned how to make their message land. They spoke with timing, with clarity, with purpose. And people listened.

That skill carried forward. In business settings now with presentations, team discussions, client conversations, Jamie's voice is one of the most valuable tools they bring. Not because they say the most, but because they know how to say *what matters*, when it matters, and how to make it resonate.

Jamie learned what many professionals never do: communication is less about what you say and more about what is heard. It's about creating alignment, building trust, and moving people toward action. And it starts by having something worth saying, and saying it well.

THE ROLE OF COMMUNICATION IN ATHLETIC SUCCESS

In sports, your ability to communicate can make or break a performance. Whether you are calling out a play, taking in a coach's feedback, or working with teammates on the field, your success depends on clear, confident, and timely communication. You have learned how to speak up, listen closely, and adjust your message depending on the situation. These are not just game-day skills—they are leadership skills, and they matter just as much in business.

In the professional world, communication is one of the most powerful tools you bring to the table. It helps you build relationships, lead teams, influence decisions, and open doors to new opportunities. Whether you are writing emails, presenting ideas, running a meeting, or navigating a one-on-one conversation, your ability to express yourself with clarity and purpose sets you apart. Just like in sports, professionals who communicate with precision and respect are the ones who move their teams forward.

On the field, communication is the glue that holds a team together. You have already seen how one miscue can lead to a missed opportunity—or even a loss. You have also seen how great communication can elevate a team's performance. You have practiced giving clear directions, reading body language, and staying composed under pressure. You have learned how to tailor your message to fit the moment, whether you are rallying a teammate, speaking to the media, or checking in with a coach. Athletes understand:

→ **Clear communication leads to better outcomes.** Whether it's a play on the field or a strategy in practice, athletes know that miscommunication can lead to failure, and clarity is crucial for success.

→ **Listening is just as important as speaking.** To succeed as a team, athletes need to listen carefully to their coaches, teammates, and even their own bodies.

→ **Nonverbal communication is vital.** In sports, body language, facial expressions, and even tone of voice can communicate just as much, if not more, than words themselves.

→ **Adaptation of the message.** Athletes must adjust their communication style depending on the audience, whether it's motivating a teammate or explaining strategy to a coach.

→ **Feedback is essential for growth.** Communication involves not just expressing thoughts but also receiving and acting on feedback to improve.

These communication skills are not limited to sports. They are exactly what the professional world needs. When you bring the same focus, intention, and adaptability to your conversations at work, you become the kind of communicator who gets results and the kind of teammate everyone wants to follow.

HOW COMMUNICATION TRANSLATES TO BUSINESS SUCCESS

"I have a voice, and I'm going to use it—not just for me, but for the people who need to be heard."

— *LeBron James*

LeBron James may be known for his dominance on the court, but what truly sets him apart is how he communicates— under pressure, across teams, and far beyond the game itself. Whether it's calling plays mid-drive or navigating billion-dollar brand deals, LeBron has developed a rare ability: he speaks with purpose, clarity, and impact.

On the floor, he's a conductor. His voice organizes a defense, guides younger teammates, and delivers real-time adjustments with authority. Former coaches and teammates say it's not just his talent that makes others better—it's how clearly and confidently he communicates expectations. No wasted words. No confusion. Just direction.

But LeBron's communication style didn't stop at the buzzer. Off the court, he's built a media company, led education initiatives, and spoken on race, politics, and equity—all while navigating the spotlight with remarkable control. He knows when to speak, how to speak, and what each moment demands. When he launched *Uninterrupted*, a platform giving athletes their own storytelling space, he was communicating a deeper message: that voice is power, and athletes don't have to wait to be handed a microphone.

In business, in advocacy, and in every team he's led,

LeBron has shown that communication isn't just about speaking clearly—it's about understanding the moment, the audience, and the outcome. He doesn't talk to impress. He talks to align, to focus, to lead.

In a world full of noise, LeBron James reminds us that great communicators aren't the loudest—they're the most intentional.

WHY COMMUNICATION IS A KEY DIFFERENTIATOR IN THE WORKPLACE

In business, poor communication can lead to confusion, missed opportunities, and broken trust. But strong communicators—like you—have the power to influence outcomes, strengthen relationships, and drive results. Just as you relied on clear communication to win games and grow as an athlete, you will rely on that same skill to lead teams, collaborate across departments, and deliver results in your career. When you express your ideas with clarity, listen with intention, and adapt your message to fit the moment, you become a professional others can count on.

For hiring managers, an athlete's background signals:

→ Receptiveness to feedback
→ Active listeners
→ Articulate messaging

The best communicators are those who deliver messages with clarity and confidence while truly listening to others and responding with thoughtfulness. You already know what that looks like. You adjusted your tone in the locker room, stayed composed when emotions ran high, and responded to coaching with focus instead of frustration. In your professional life, your ability to adapt your communication style will set you apart. Whether you are presenting to executives, collaborating with colleagues, or navigating a tough conversation with a client, your emotional intelligence and flexibility will help you connect, resolve conflict, and lead with impact.

THE PSYCHOLOGICAL BENEFITS OF COMMUNICATION

The ability to communicate effectively gives you a sense of confidence and control. As an athlete, you saw firsthand how clear communication built trust, improved team chemistry, and elevated performance. In the professional world, that same skill will open doors. When you express yourself clearly, influence others with your words, and handle tough conversations with composure, you position yourself as someone who can lead, connect, and deliver results.

The psychological benefits of communication include:

→ **Increased confidence**—Expressing ideas, giving presentations, and responding to feedback become easier with strong communication skills.

→ **Reduced stress**—Clear communication helps resolve misunderstandings quickly and facilitates smoother problem-solving.

→ **Stronger relationships**—Open, honest communication fosters trust, strengthens teamwork, and enhances collaboration.

→ **Enhanced problem-solving and creativity**—Effectively exchanging ideas and perspectives leads to more innovative solutions.

BUILDING A CULTURE OF COMMUNICATION IN THE WORKPLACE

Organizations that prioritize communication create environments where collaboration, innovation, and growth come naturally. As someone who has thrived in team huddles, debriefs, and high-pressure moments, you understand that strong communication is the foundation of success. You bring valuable skills like listening intently, giving and receiving feedback, and expressing yourself clearly that can elevate any team culture.

Look for organizations that invest in communication development. These are places where you can continue growing in areas like writing, presenting, and one-on-one connection. Strong environments also encourage open dialogue across all levels of the team. When leaders are accessible and transparent, and when ideas are exchanged freely, trust is built and collaboration improves.

Pay attention to how teams give and receive feedback. A healthy communication culture includes regular, constructive conversations that help everyone improve. If departments work closely together and openly share resources and insights, it is a sign of a workplace that values openness and teamwork over silos and internal competition.

When you bring your communication strengths into this kind of environment, you become a connector. You bring clarity and direction while helping others feel seen, heard, and understood. You help foster a culture where people thrive, goals stay aligned, and progress moves forward.

CORPORATE APPLICATION OF COMMUNICATION
Writing Professional Emails and Reports

Just as you needed to communicate clearly with teammates and coaches in high pressure moments, you now need to do the same in writing. In the business world, emails, reports, and proposals are how decisions get made and goals move forward. Writing with clarity, professionalism, and purpose ensures that your ideas are understood, your action steps are clear, and your voice has an impact. The same focus you brought to pregame strategy talks now applies to how you communicate through words on the page. It is not just about what you say, it is about how you say it.

How athletes apply this:

- ✔ Communicating clearly and concisely when providing feedback or summarizing a strategy.
- ✔ Crafting well-structured reports or summaries of performance, similar to how they analyze games or practice sessions.

✓ Using a tone appropriate for the context, whether it's motivating teammates or addressing sponsors or executives.

✓ Avoiding jargon or overly complex language, ensuring that the intended message is accessible to a wide audience.

Delivering Compelling Presentations and Pitches

As an athlete, you have likely been asked to speak to the media, give postgame interviews, address your teammates, or share your story with fans or sponsors. These moments helped you build public speaking skills and learn how to deliver a clear and compelling message under pressure. In business, those same skills set you apart. Whether you are pitching an idea to a client, leading a team meeting, or presenting to executives, your ability to engage an audience, communicate with confidence, and inspire action will shape how others see your leadership. Great presenters do more than share information. They influence, persuade, and leave a lasting impression. Their words connect with the audience, not just through content, but through clarity, confidence, and authenticity.

How athletes apply this:

✓ Speaking confidently in front of teammates, coaches, and fans, which builds public speaking skills that can be transferred to corporate pitches.

✓ Presenting performance data or game strategies in a clear, concise, and engaging way.

- Using stories or examples to make ideas more relatable and memorable, much like how athletes often use game highlights to illustrate points.

- Keeping the message focused and ensuring key takeaways are clear, similar to how athletes focus on essential game strategies or tactical adjustments.

Effectively Listening and Responding in Meetings

Communication is a two-way street. As an athlete, you learned to listen with purpose by taking in feedback, understanding different perspectives, and reading situations in real time. That same skill is essential in the workplace, where active listening builds trust, strengthens collaboration, and leads to clearer decisions. But communication is not just about listening. It also means knowing when and how to speak up. Whether you are challenging a decision, raising a concern, or offering feedback, doing so with professionalism and emotional intelligence shows leadership. Constructive feedback that is delivered with empathy and clarity helps others grow and strengthens team performance. Speaking up and listening well are both vital parts of being an effective communicator and teammate.

How athletes apply this:

- Actively listening during team huddles, practice feedback sessions, or one-on-one meetings with coaches, and responding with thoughtful questions or comments.

✔ Responding to feedback or criticism in a way that shows respect and a desire to improve.

✔ Understanding nonverbal cues from teammates and coaches, such as body language, tone of voice, and facial expressions, to gauge how messages are being received.

✔ Collaborating with teammates to solve problems, as they would in a business meeting when brainstorming ideas or addressing challenges.

✔ Speaking up when something doesn't feel right, using respectful language and clear reasoning to express concerns or disagreement.

✔ Giving constructive feedback that is specific, focused on behavior rather than personality, and intended to help people succeed.

📋 Practice Plan

Great communication is not just about talking. It is about listening, observing, and responding with intention. As an athlete, you have learned to communicate clearly under pressure, take in tough feedback, and read nonverbal cues when words were not enough. Whether it was in a huddle, during a one on one with a coach, or while working through a conflict with a teammate, you have already been practicing many of the same skills you will rely on in the workplace.

Use the questions below to reflect on your experiences as a communicator in sport:

→ Recall a time when there was a miscommunication between myself and a coach or teammate. What caused the misunderstanding? How did I work through that conflict? What approach helped clarify or repair the situation?

→ When did I receive tough feedback or criticism, and how did I respond in the moment? Did I ask clarifying questions, stay open, or shut down?

→ How have I demonstrated active listening during team huddles or one-on-one meetings? What habits helped me stay engaged? Have I ever relied on body language, tone, or facial expressions to read a situation—especially when emotions were high?

→ What's a time I contributed to a team solution by clearly expressing an idea or helping others communicate better?

Now think forward. How can these same communication habits serve you in business? What does it mean to be an active listener in a meeting or during feedback with a manager? How could your ability to read the room, ask thoughtful questions, or stay calm during conflict give you an edge? What might it look like to speak up when something does not feel right, while still being respectful and professional? How can you offer constructive feedback to a teammate or colleague in a way that supports growth rather than discourages it? Communication is more than what you say. It is how you connect, how you lead, and how you help others succeed.

Grab a pen—or open a new document—and start unpacking the ways you already know how to listen, adapt, and lead with your words.

Postgame Recap

Communication is one of the most essential skills in both athletics and business. Just as you had to communicate with teammates, coaches, and the media, you will need to express ideas clearly, deliver compelling presentations, and listen actively in your professional life. The ability to communicate effectively fosters collaboration, trust, and problem-solving, helping individuals and organizations achieve success.

When you master communication on the field, you are already preparing for your next arena. Your ability to influence, engage, and collaborate will help you thrive in the workplace. Whether you are writing professional emails, delivering presentations, or participating in meaningful discussions, strong communication skills will allow you to build relationships, drive results, and make a lasting impact.

7

LEADERSHIP

INSPIRING AND GUIDING OTHERS

BEHIND THE BENCH

Jamie didn't always lead with speeches. They led with habits. By their senior year, the team didn't need to be told who to follow. It was obvious. Jamie showed up first, left last, and treated every rep like it counted. They held themselves accountable, even when no one was watching. And over time, that became the culture.

There wasn't a single "leadership moment." It was the string of a hundred small ones, such as pulling a younger teammate aside for extra drills, resetting the tone after a sloppy practice, walking into every game with the same quiet focus that said: we're here to compete.

People didn't follow Jamie because they demanded it. They followed because Jamie's presence made them better.

That kind of leadership carried forward. Today, in high-pressure business settings, Jamie doesn't chase authority, they earn trust. They build belief through consistency. When stress spikes, Jamie stays level. When things go wrong, they take ownership. When someone new joins the team, Jamie makes sure they feel like they belong. Leadership, as Jamie shows, isn't about volume. It's about standards. It's about raising your own bar and in doing so, raising everyone else's.

THE ROLE OF LEADERSHIP IN ATHLETIC SUCCESS

Leadership is an essential quality for success in both sports and business. In athletics, leadership is developed through the ability to motivate teammates, make critical decisions under pressure, and lead by example. Whether as captains, mentors, or vocal leaders on the field, athletes are frequently placed in positions where they must inspire, guide, and support others to achieve collective success.

The same leadership skills that athletes develop during their careers are highly valued in the corporate world, where companies seek employees who can influence, inspire, and guide teams toward achieving shared objectives.

In the workplace, leadership is about more than holding a position of authority. It is about being someone others can look up to, trust, and follow. Corporate leaders are expected to set clear objectives, make decisions that drive progress, and motivate others to perform at their best.

For former athletes, the transition to leadership roles can be a natural one. The teamwork, accountability, and communication skills developed in sports serve as a strong foundation for leadership in any professional environment.

In sports, leadership is not limited to a specific role or title. While team captains often take on the responsibility of guiding the team, leadership can also emerge in less formal ways. Athletes lead by setting a positive example, motivating others through their actions, and offering support when it is needed most. A leader in sports is someone who rises to the occasion, especially in tough situations, and brings out the best in their teammates.

Athletes understand:

→ **Leadership is about influence, not authority.** The best leaders inspire their teammates through their actions and words, not through a title.

→ **Leading by example matters.** Athletes who give their best effort in practice, exhibit discipline, and maintain a positive attitude inspire others to follow suit.

→ **Teamwork is essential.** A true leader elevates the performance of the entire team, fostering a sense of unity and shared purpose.

→ **Adaptability is a key.** Leadership isn't about one-size-fits-all solutions; it's about adapting to different situations and knowing how to engage with people based on their strengths and weaknesses.

→ **Mentorship matters.** Effective leaders guide others, providing support, advice, and encouragement, both on and off the field.

Leadership in sports involves more than just taking charge. It requires you to inspire others, make decisions that benefit the team, and ensure that everyone is working toward the same goal. These are the qualities that have made you a strong presence on the field, and they are the same qualities that will make you an exceptional leader in your career. You already know how to unite a group behind a shared vision, how to lead with integrity, and how to step up when it matters most.

HOW LEADERSHIP TRANSLATES TO BUSINESS SUCCESS

"You can't accomplish anything without the help of others, and you can't lead others without earning their trust."
— *Tom Brady*

Tom Brady wasn't the most gifted athlete in his draft class. He wasn't fast. He didn't have a cannon for an arm. He was picked 199th overall in the 2000 NFL Draft, six quarterbacks were chosen before him. But what those teams didn't see was the quality that would define his career: his ability to lead.

From his early days with the New England Patriots to his final seasons with the Tampa Bay Buccaneers, Brady proved that leadership isn't about hype, it's about consistency. He led by example, showing up earlier, studying harder, and holding himself to a higher standard than anyone else in the room. He didn't demand respect. He earned it.

Brady's teammates describe him not as the loudest voice in the huddle, but as the most focused. He expected precision—not perfection, but effort with intent. He learned everyone's name, knew what made them tick, and challenged them to raise their level. And he backed it all up on the field, leading 55 game-winning drives in his career, often in moments when the stakes couldn't be higher.

Off the field, Brady has approached life after football with the same discipline and intentionality that made him great on it. He didn't wait until retirement to start thinking strategically. While still winning Super Bowls, he was building the foundation for a second act—one centered around performance, longevity, and mindset. He co-founded TB12, a wellness and training company that challenges traditional strength models in favor of pliability, nutrition, and recovery. The brand isn't just about fitness, it's about a philosophy he lived every day, and it reflects his deep belief in preparation and personal optimization.

Brady also launched 199 Productions, a content company named after his infamous draft number, with a mission to tell underdog stories and reshape narratives in sports and beyond. He's not just lending his name, he's helping shape the message, the team, and the vision. Like his game-winning drives, these business moves are carefully timed, smartly positioned, and always backed by a long-term strategy.

Even in media appearances and brand partnerships, Brady communicates with clarity, restraint, and focus. He's not loud, but he's always deliberate. Every word, every endorsement, every initiative feels aligned with the identity he's crafted over decades: competitive, prepared, forward-thinking. He understands that leadership doesn't stop when the clock runs out. It evolves.

Tom Brady's story proves that great leaders aren't always the most naturally gifted. They're the ones who show up every day, guide others with purpose, and never stop setting the standard on the field, in the locker room, or at the head of the table.

WHY LEADERSHIP IS A KEY DIFFERENTIATOR IN THE WORKPLACE

In the corporate world, leadership is one of the most sought-after skills. Companies are always looking for individuals who can influence others, create a positive team dynamic, and drive results. While technical skills matter, it is leadership that often separates good professionals from great ones. You are someone who can lead, inspire, and motivate others, and that is exactly what puts you on a path to rise to the top.

An athlete's leadership experience is beneficial for:

- ✔ Creating a positive team dynamic
- ✔ Ensuring that everyone is working toward the same goal
- ✔ Fostering a sense of unity

You are uniquely prepared to lead in the business world because you have faced pressure, made quick decisions, and stayed focused through adversity. You have worked with different personalities, balanced competing priorities, and stayed calm when others looked to you for direction. These are not just sports experiences—they are leadership credentials.

In your professional life, leadership is about more than just managing tasks. It is about creating a culture of trust, collaboration, and accountability. Your ability to guide others, inspire belief, and hold high standards will make you the kind of leader people want to follow.

THE PSYCHOLOGICAL BENEFITS OF LEADERSHIP

Leadership also brings powerful psychological benefits. When you lead effectively, you strengthen your confidence, build self-belief, and develop emotional intelligence. As you guide and support others, you often discover a deeper sense of purpose and fulfillment within yourself. Through leadership, you cultivate the mental toughness and resilience needed to stay calm under pressure, navigate challenges, and make tough decisions with clarity. These qualities not only help you elevate your team but also help you grow into the strongest version of yourself.

The psychological benefits of leadership include:

→ **Increased self-confidence**—Successfully guiding others and making strategic decisions reinforces trust in one's abilities.

→ **Improved emotional intelligence**—Understanding and managing both personal and team emotions enhances relationships and decision-making.

→ **Enhanced problem-solving abilities**—Constant decision-making and adaptability sharpen critical thinking and problem-solving skills.

→ **Greater sense of purpose and fulfillment**—Leading others provides the opportunity to make a meaningful impact, fostering motivation and personal satisfaction.

BUILDING A CULTURE OF LEADERSHIP IN THE WORKPLACE

Organizations that foster leadership create environments where people are empowered to take initiative, contribute ideas, and share responsibility for success. You know from experience that leadership is not about barking orders. It is about setting an example, building trust, and helping others rise to the occasion. In the workplace, strong leadership cultures value people who step up, guide others, and take ownership regardless of their job title.

Look for environments where leadership is not limited to senior roles. The best companies encourage everyone to take the lead when the moment calls for it. Pay attention to whether they invest in mentorship, coaching, and growth opportunities that help individuals develop their leadership skills. Great cultures also make a habit of recognizing those who support, motivate, and inspire others, not just those who hit performance metrics.

A strong leadership culture also feels collaborative. People care about the team's success, not just their own. They feel seen, heard, and trusted to make meaningful contributions. When you step into an organization like that, your experience as a teammate and leader becomes a powerful asset. You help set a tone where leadership is not a title—it is a mindset that strengthens everyone around you.

CORPORATE APPLICATION OF LEADERSHIP
Leading Team Projects and Motivating Colleagues

In both sports and business, leadership is about bringing out the best in others. As a leader, you know how to motivate your teammates, help them push through challenges, and guide them toward a shared goal. Just like you did during tough games, you can step up in the workplace to inspire your colleagues to give their best effort, even when the pressure is high. Your ability to lead with energy, empathy, and focus will set the tone for those around you and drive your team to succeed.

How athletes apply this:

- ✔ Encouraging teammates during difficult times, much like a leader would motivate colleagues during high-pressure projects.

- ✔ Maintaining a positive attitude, even when facing setbacks, to help the team stay focused and energized.

✔ Recognizing individual strengths and finding ways to harness them to benefit the team as a whole.

Effectively Communicating a Vision and Setting Clear Objectives

Leadership is about more than just managing tasks. It is about communicating a vision that inspires others to follow. As an athlete, you learned how to communicate game plans, strategies, and goals to your teammates. In business, the same principle applies. As a leader, you have the power to clearly share your organization's objectives and make sure everyone around you is aligned and energized to achieve them. When you lead with clarity and purpose, you give people a reason to believe in the mission and commit fully to the journey.

How athletes apply this:

✔ Setting clear goals for themselves and their team, and ensuring everyone understands their roles and responsibilities.

✔ Communicating a shared vision that excites and motivates others, much like a coach setting the tone for a game or season.

✔ Listening to feedback from teammates, colleagues, and mentors, and adjusting strategies accordingly to improve outcomes.

Making Strategic Decisions that Benefit the Entire Organization

In both sports and business, you will often face decisions that affect the success of the entire team or organization. These choices require foresight, thoughtful analysis, and the ability to weigh short-term demands against long-term goals. Just like deciding on the right strategy for a big game, making strong business decisions means considering what is best for everyone involved. As a leader, your ability to step up, think ahead, and take responsibility for those choices is what sets you apart and earns the trust of those around you.

How athletes apply this:

- ✔ Analyzing the situation and making decisions based on the collective needs of the team or organization, rather than individual preferences.
- ✔ Being willing to take calculated risks in order to achieve greater success for the team or company.
- ✔ Demonstrating the confidence to make tough calls when necessary, and taking responsibility for those decisions.

📋 Practice Plan

Leadership is not just about being in charge. It is about earning trust, guiding others through challenges, and creating an environment where everyone has the opportunity to succeed. As an athlete, you have already stepped into leadership, sometimes with a title and often without one. Whether you were a captain or someone who led through your actions, you inspired teammates, stayed composed under pressure, and helped your group stay focused when adversity hit. Those moments shaped you into the kind of leader who can make a lasting impact far beyond the field. Use the questions below to reflect on how you have led others in sport and how those same qualities can shape your professional future.

→ Can I recall a time when I helped lead a team through a tough situation or toward a shared goal? What obstacle did we face?

→ How did I get buy-in from others? What did I say or do to get the team aligned and motivated?

→ What actions did I take to keep the group focused, especially during setbacks or high-stress moments?

→ How did I recognize and use the strengths of individual teammates to help the whole team succeed?

→ What was the outcome of my leadership? How did the team grow or improve as a result?

Now look ahead. In your career, you will have opportunities to lead in many different ways. That could mean keeping a project on track, mentoring a new teammate, or staying steady during a stressful deadline. Leadership in business often mirrors leadership in sport. It means encouraging others when things get tough, recognizing strengths in people and putting them in positions to succeed, and staying positive and focused regardless of the outcome. The habits you built through athletics, like staying composed, earning trust, and rallying a team, are powerful tools in any workplace. You already know how to lead.

The next step is choosing to lead in a new environment with the same conviction and care you brought to every practice and game. What leadership qualities did you develop in sport, such as resilience, communication, or encouragement, that could make a real impact in your next role? Ask yourself how you might use your leadership instincts to motivate a team during a tight deadline, navigate workplace conflict, or bring out the best in others.

Grab a pen—or open a new document—and write it out.

Postgame Recap

Leadership is a powerful skill that can drive success both in sports and in business. The ability to inspire, guide, and motivate others is what separates great leaders from the rest. As an athlete, you have developed leadership through your experiences in teamwork, communication, and decision making under pressure. You already know how to stay composed in tough moments, bring people together, and push others to perform at their best.

By using your leadership qualities, you can make a real impact in your workplace. You have what it takes to help teams stay focused, solve problems, and grow through challenges. Leadership is not about having a title. It is about influence, vision, and the belief that your example can move others to greatness. You have done that in sport. Now it is your time to lead in the next chapter of your life.

8

TEAMWORK

THRIVING IN A COLLABORATIVE ENVIRONMENT

BEHIND THE BENCH

There was a stretch early in Jamie's career where they were trying to do everything. Leading the team in scoring, covering for defensive mistakes, pushing the pace, keeping the energy up. It came from a good place. They cared. They wanted to win. But they hadn't learned yet what it really meant to play *within a team*.

I remember one game where it all fell apart. Jamie forced shots, missed rotations, and by the second half, the team looked disjointed. We lost badly, not because of effort, but because no one was playing together. After the game, Jamie didn't make excuses. They just sat with it.

That week in film, something clicked. Jamie started seeing the game differently. They noticed how one player's cut opened up another's shot. How a screen set two seconds early created space down low. How the game changed when everyone trusted the system, not just their instincts. They began to shift. They talked more on defense. Gave up a good shot for a great one. Celebrated a teammate's bucket like it was their own. And the team followed. Jamie didn't lose their edge. They just learned how to channel it into the group. Their energy became contagious. Their decisions became unselfish. Their impact grew, not because they were doing more, but because they were helping everyone do better.

That experience shaped how they now work in high performing business teams. Whether it's launching a product or managing a cross functional project, Jamie knows how to make the people around them sharper. They listen. They pass credit. They fill gaps. They are clear about their role, and just as clear about supporting others in theirs. Teamwork isn't just about getting along. It's about creating chemistry, sharing ownership, and trusting that when everyone plays their part, the whole becomes stronger than the sum of its stats. Jamie learned that on the court. And they live it every day.

THE ROLE OF TEAMWORK IN ATHLETIC SUCCESS

No athlete succeeds alone. Whether you played on a team or relied on a coach, teammates, and support staff, you know that success is built through collaboration. In sports, individual achievements matter, but it is the team that ultimately determines the outcome.

This same truth applies in the corporate world. Teamwork is not just a nice bonus. It is essential. Professionals must be able to work with a wide range of people, contribute to group goals, and navigate different personalities and dynamics to succeed together. Teamwork is more than just cooperating. It is about building an environment where every person can contribute, grow, and thrive.

As a former athlete, stepping into a collaborative workplace often feels natural. You have already learned how to be part of something bigger than yourself. You understand the importance of each person's role and how their contributions drive the group forward. That ability to function as part of a team, communicate clearly, and collaborate effectively is one of your greatest assets. It is a skill that reaches far beyond sport and holds value in any professional space.

In sports, teamwork is everything. A team is only as strong as its least prepared member. You learned early that real success requires support, sacrifice, and unity. Whether you were on the field, the court, or the track, you relied on your teammates. You trusted them to do their part just as they trusted you. Teamwork is about balancing your individual performance with the needs of the group and pulling together toward a common mission.

Athletes understand:

→ **Collaboration is key.** While individual brilliance may shine in a moment, it's the collective effort of the team that secures long-term success.

93

→ **Everyone has a role to play.** Whether it's the star player or the supportive role player, each person's contributions are vital.

→ **Communication is essential.** Clear, open communication helps teams function smoothly, whether in practice, a game, or during a strategic discussion.

→ **Adaptability is important.** Teams are dynamic, and athletes must be flexible, able to adjust to changes in strategy or personnel at a moment's notice.

→ **Support and trust matter.** Trusting your teammates, and knowing they trust you, fosters an environment where everyone can contribute their best.

Teamwork in sports taught you how to function as part of a unit, how to trust your teammates, and how to give your best for a goal bigger than yourself. You know what it means to rely on others and to be the one others can count on. That mindset, that ability to contribute to something greater, is exactly what makes you stand out in the professional world.

HOW TEAMWORK TRANSLATES TO BUSINESS SUCCESS

"A team is a group that trusts each other. And if they trust each other, they'll share the ball—and the success."
— *Dean Smith*

I had the privilege of working for Coach Dean Smith. And I can tell you firsthand: everything you've heard about his emphasis on team over self, about his obsession with doing things the right way, about how he lived the motto—Play Hard, Play Smart, Play Together—is absolutely true. But it was the third part, *Play Together*, that defined everything.

Coach Smith didn't just build basketball teams. He built cultures rooted in trust, discipline, and shared accountability. He made sure every player, from the stars to the last man on the bench, understood that their role mattered—and that ego had no place in a Carolina jersey. I saw how he created an environment where unselfishness wasn't just encouraged—it was expected. Point to the passer. Share the credit. Make the extra pass. Do your job, not for applause, but because the team depends on it.

I watched practices that felt more like leadership labs than workouts. Coach didn't just teach plays—he taught awareness. Where's your teammate? Who's in better position? What's the right decision *for the team*? Everything was about connection, timing, and putting others in a position to succeed. He wasn't just building better basketball players—he was building better teammates, and better people.

I've carried those lessons with me into every professional environment I've stepped into, especially within the Fortune 500 companies where I've led teams, launched initiatives, and helped shape culture. What I learned from Coach Smith became my foundation: clarity of roles, mutual accountability, and above all, trust. Whether I was building a new division or stepping into an underperforming team, I didn't start with strategy decks or incentive plans. I started by creating a culture where people were seen, valued, and aligned—where they understood that their individual success depended on the team's success. We built systems that rewarded collaboration, we celebrated the "assist," and we made it clear that no one wins unless we all do. Just like Coach's teams, the goal wasn't to outshine—it was to out-execute, together.

Coach Smith didn't just teach basketball. He taught how to thrive inside a system. How to lead with humility. How to commit to the group and elevate everyone around you. *Play Together* wasn't just part of a motto—it was a way of life. And once you've experienced it, you never build a team the same way again.

WHY TEAMWORK IS A KEY DIFFERENTIATOR IN THE WORKPLACE

In today's fast paced and interconnected business world, teamwork is a key differentiator for high performing organizations. When you prioritize collaboration, mutual respect, and open communication, you contribute to outcomes that outperform those of teams that do not. Teamwork leads to innovation, faster problem solving, and more efficient execution. You know that success is rarely achieved in isolation and that the collective effort of a group leads to greater achievements than any one individual could accomplish alone.

Athletes have experience in:

→ Collaboration
→ Values the contributions of others
→ Strive for collective success

Your experience in competitive environments has taught you the importance of working together and supporting those around you. Whether you are collaborating on a cross functional project, contributing to a team initiative, or leading a group of colleagues, you know how to leverage the strengths of others for the collective good.

Teamwork is also the key to sustaining a positive and productive workplace culture. When you work well with others, you build a sense of unity and shared purpose that elevates job satisfaction and drives performance. Your ability to foster collaboration, adapt to different personalities, and contribute selflessly equips you to overcome challenges and help your team thrive in any professional setting.

THE PSYCHOLOGICAL BENEFITS OF TEAMWORK

The benefits of teamwork go far beyond just getting things done. When you work in a collaborative environment, you strengthen your emotional intelligence, sharpen your communication skills, and deepen your self-awareness. Being part of a supportive team helps you feel more confident and grounded in your role.

When trust is strong and relationships are built on respect, you do your best work. Team success becomes your success. That sense of shared achievement boosts morale, strengthens commitment, and makes the journey more rewarding. Teamwork not only elevates your performance but also enhances your overall sense of purpose and fulfillment in your career.

The psychological benefits of teamwork include:

→ **Improved communication skills**—Team members learn to express their thoughts clearly and listen actively to others.

→ **Greater emotional intelligence**—Engaging with colleagues and understanding different perspectives enhance empathy and interpersonal skills.

→ **Stronger sense of community**—Building relationships within a team fosters connection, support, and a shared sense of purpose.

→ **Increased job satisfaction**—Collaborative efforts lead to shared achievements, reinforcing a sense of fulfillment and accomplishment.

BUILDING A CULTURE OF TEAMWORK IN THE WORKPLACE

Organizations that promote a culture of teamwork create environments where collaboration is more than a buzzword. It is a lived value that brings people together, fuels innovation, and drives meaningful progress. In these environments, people work toward common goals, communication is open and respectful, and team achievements are recognized and celebrated. Leaders support this by removing barriers between departments, encouraging cross-functional collaboration, and giving people the space and trust to contribute their ideas.

When you look for a workplace that values teamwork, pay attention to how people interact. Do they share credit, ask for input, and listen to one another? Do teams come together across roles and functions to solve problems and get things done? Are team wins highlighted and rewarded in the same way individual success is?

As someone who has lived the reality of teamwork in sport, you bring a deep understanding of how to contribute, support others, and stay focused on the greater goal. Your presence strengthens the culture of any organization because you know that real success comes when everyone pulls in the same direction. Your ability to lead from within the team, communicate clearly, and stay united under pressure helps build high-performing groups that thrive together.

CORPORATE APPLICATION OF TEAMWORK
Collaborating with Coworkers Across Different Departments

In business, collaboration often extends beyond a single team or department. You must work with individuals from various areas of the company, each bringing their unique expertise and perspectives. Just as you collaborated with teammates, coaches, and support staff, you now engage with colleagues across different disciplines to achieve shared goals.

How athletes apply this:

- ✔ Drawing on diverse experiences to bring innovative solutions to the table, much like athletes utilize various training and skill sets to prepare for competition.

✔ Being flexible and adaptable when working with colleagues from different departments or backgrounds.

✔ Understanding the importance of each individual's contribution, whether it's from marketing, finance, or operations, and recognizing how each piece of the puzzle contributes to the overall success.

Contributing Ideas While Respecting the Input of Others

Teamwork is not just about following directions; it is about contributing to the collective effort. In sports, you often collaborated on strategies, shared insights, and made suggestions to improve team performance. Similarly, in the workplace, you must contribute ideas while respecting the perspectives and expertise of others. Collaborative environments thrive when everyone feels their voice is heard and valued.

How athletes apply this:

✔ Actively participating in team discussions, offering ideas that contribute to the team's objectives.

✔ Respecting the input and suggestions of others, understanding that every perspective has value.

✔ Balancing confidence in one's ideas with the humility to accept and integrate feedback from teammates or colleagues.

Building Relationships and Fostering a Positive Work Environment

Successful teams, both in sports and business, are built on strong relationships. You know that building trust with your teammates fosters a supportive environment where everyone can thrive. In business, your ability to develop strong relationships with colleagues, clients, and stakeholders is critical. Creating a positive, collaborative work environment is essential for sustaining high performance and morale.

How athletes apply this:

- ✔ Developing strong interpersonal relationships by showing genuine interest in teammates and colleagues, building trust and camaraderie.

- ✔ Being approachable and supportive, creating a work culture where people feel comfortable sharing ideas and asking for help.

- ✔ Encouraging a positive and inclusive work environment, just as athletes strive to maintain morale and unity during tough times.

📋 Practice Plan

Teamwork is one of the most fundamental aspects of being an athlete. You have trained with teammates, relied on them during competition, and figured out how to function together under pressure. But teamwork is not always smooth. It takes real skill to collaborate, communicate, and stay focused on a shared goal—especially when personalities clash or feedback is not well received. This exercise will help you reflect on the moments that built your ability to work with others and prepare you to bring that same mindset into any team setting in your career.

Consider the following questions:

→ When was a time I had to work with someone I didn't naturally get along with? How did I handle it, and what helped us move forward together?

→ What role did I often play on a team—organizer, encourager, strategist, problem-solver? How did that contribute to group success?

→ How did I help my team stay focused or motivated during a tough stretch—on the field, in training, or in competition?

→ When have I helped a teammate succeed by stepping up, stepping back, or adjusting my role to fit what the team needed?

→ How did I build trust within a team—even when things weren't going smoothly?

Now look ahead to your professional life. Working in teams is just as central to business as it is to sport. Whether it is in a staff meeting, a project group, or a collaborative brainstorm, the ability to contribute, listen, adapt, and find common ground will set you apart. You have already done this in buses, in locker rooms, on practice fields, and in games that mattered. You have learned to work toward something bigger than yourself. Teamwork in the professional world is simply the next expression of what you have already practiced for years.

Grab a pen—or open a new document—and write about how you've shown up as a teammate—and how you'll continue to do so, wherever you go next.

Postgame Recap

Teamwork is a cornerstone of both athletic and business success. Your ability to collaborate, contribute ideas, and work toward common goals is essential for high performance. You have already honed these skills on the field, and now they are one of your greatest assets in the corporate world. By drawing on your experiences in collaboration, communication, and relationship-building, you can thrive in team-oriented environments and help your organization achieve collective success. Teamwork is not just about working together—it is about inspiring those around you, building trust, and striving for shared excellence. When you apply the teamwork principles you learned in sports to your professional life, you become an invaluable contributor to any team or organization.

9

EMOTIONAL INTELLIGENCE

UNDERSTANDING AND MANAGING EMOTIONS

BEHIND THE BENCH

Jamie had always been intense, especially early on. Competitive. Locked in. That edge had fueled their rise through every early morning workout, late night film session, and high pressure game. But intensity does not always translate to composure. And for a while, that gap showed up at the worst moments. I remember a game where the officiating was awful. Missed calls, uneven whistles, frustration building on every possession. Jamie snapped. Threw their hands up at a ref. Barked at a teammate after a turnover. Their stats were solid, but their energy was off. We lost. And in the locker room afterward, Jamie sat there silent, knowing it.

What came next wasn't dramatic. It was subtle. Jamie started asking different questions. Not just about strategy, but about presence. They began watching how emotions moved through the team. Who got quiet after a mistake. Who tightened up under pressure. Who needed encouragement in the middle of a rough stretch. They worked on it in themselves first. Breathing exercises. Self-talk routines. Pausing before responding. Reframing setbacks mid game. They learned how to stay level, not by shutting off emotion, but by staying in control of it. And then they used that calm to center others. I saw it in moments where the team used to spiral. A missed assignment, a bad run, a tough call, and Jamie would step in. Not with noise, but with presence. A look. A word. A reset. The game would slow down. The group would settle.

That kind of awareness followed them to the boardroom. In meetings. In conflict. In pressure filled environments where others were reactive, Jamie stayed grounded. Not because they didn't feel the weight, but because they had learned how to carry it. Emotional intelligence is not about hiding emotion. It is about recognizing it, regulating it, and responding with intention. And for Jamie, it became one of the most powerful tools in their leadership toolbox. Not loud. Not flashy. Just steady in the storm.

THE ROLE OF EMOTIONAL INTELLIGENCE IN ATHLETIC SUCCESS

In the heat of competition, you face intense pressure. Whether it is a championship game, a critical decision, or a moment when things do not go your way, emotions can surge. But you know that managing your emotions is just as vital as physical preparation. You train yourself to control stress, stay centered, and channel your focus so you can perform at your highest level. You also learn to recognize the emotions of your teammates, to offer support, and to lift each other up when it matters most. Perhaps most importantly, you learn that strength isn't just about pushing through alone. It's also about knowing when to ask for help. Reaching out, leaning on a teammate, or seeking guidance from a coach is not a sign of weakness; it's a sign of maturity, trust, and emotional intelligence.

In the professional world, emotional intelligence is just as powerful. It is your ability to recognize what you are feeling, understand why you feel that way, and respond with intention. It is also about reading the room, understanding others, and building strong relationships through empathy and respect. Emotional intelligence is the edge that sets great leaders and teammates apart. It helps you stay calm under pressure, resolve conflicts with confidence, and navigate tough conversations without losing your composure. It also gives you the self-awareness and humility to acknowledge when you're overwhelmed and the courage to ask for support when needed. This builds trust and psychological safety on any team.

Just like in sport, emotional intelligence is often the difference between success and struggle in your career. When you keep your emotions in check, stay focused under stress, and lift others with your energy, you lead by example. Whether you are bouncing back from a setback, delivering feedback with empathy, or supporting a colleague through a challenge, your emotional intelligence allows you to make a meaningful impact—on your team, your culture, and your results. You have already practiced this in your athletic life. Now, you are ready to apply it in the workplace.

Athletes understand:

→ **Self-awareness is key.** Understanding their emotional state allows athletes to regulate their feelings and adjust their mindset accordingly.

→ **Asking for help is a strength.** Athletes know that reaching out for support can be the key to growth, recovery, and sustained performance, whether from a coach, a teammate, or a mental health professional.

→ **Stress management is essential.** In high-pressure moments, athletes need to stay calm and composed to perform at their best.

→ **Empathy enhances teamwork.** Understanding and supporting teammates' emotions builds stronger team dynamics, which translates to better overall performance.

→ **Emotions influence decisions.** Recognizing the impact of emotions on decision-making helps athletes make more rational choices in crucial moments.

→ **Resilience is rooted in emotional intelligence.** Athletes bounce back from setbacks more effectively when they can manage their emotions and focus on recovery.

Your ability to control emotions, empathize with others, and respond effectively in high pressure situations is what helps you succeed both individually and as part of a team. You've already proven you can stay composed when the stakes are high and others are counting on you. That emotional strength, including the ability to ask for help when you need it, will continue to set you apart as you navigate the challenges and opportunities of your professional journey.

HOW EMOTIONAL INTELLIGENCE TRANSLATES TO BUSINESS SUCCESS

"You have eight people giving everything they have, and you can feel when something's off—before they even say a word."
— Mary Whipple

Mary Whipple didn't pull an oar. She didn't generate any physical power. But as the coxswain of the U.S. Women's Eight—two-time Olympic gold medalists—she steered not just the boat, but the *emotional energy* of the team. Rowing is grueling. Races are won by fractions of seconds. There's no time for long speeches or corrections in the middle of a sprint. The coxswain must read the rhythm, feel the shifts in focus or frustration, and make real-time adjustments—not just to direction, but to the *tone* of the crew.

Whipple mastered this. She didn't just bark commands— she communicated with precision, pacing, and empathy. She could sense when a rower was off—not because they said something, but because of a change in rhythm, tension, or breath. Her emotional intelligence helped her know when to push, when to calm, when to call for power, and when to simply let the team flow. She aligned not just physical movement, but mental state.

After her athletic career, Whipple began working with corporate teams and leadership groups, teaching that the same principles apply in business. The most effective leaders, she says, are tuned in—not reactive, but responsive. They manage stress by staying grounded. They communicate not just clearly, but *compassionately*. And they understand that teams perform best when people feel *seen*, even in silence.

Mary Whipple's story reminds us that emotional intelligence isn't abstract—it's operational. It's what allows leaders to manage energy, defuse tension, and unlock performance in the moments that matter most.

WHY EMOTIONAL INTELLIGENCE IS A KEY DIFFERENTIATOR IN THE WORKPLACE

While technical skills and expertise matter, your emotional intelligence is what truly sets you apart in the workplace. When you can navigate complex social dynamics, build strong relationships with colleagues, and stay calm under pressure, you become someone others want to work with and follow. These are the skills that drive real influence and success in any industry.

Employers look for individuals like athletes who:

→ Manage their emotions

→ Work well with others

→ Contribute to a positive, productive work environment

As an athlete, you already know how to manage your emotions, read the room, and stay focused when everything is on the line. You have spent years building awareness of your own mindset and supporting the emotional needs of your teammates. These same skills will serve you powerfully in your career. Emotional intelligence is not just a business buzzword. It is your competitive edge in leadership, collaboration, and long-term success.

THE PSYCHOLOGICAL BENEFITS OF EMOTIONAL INTELLIGENCE

Beyond its professional applications, emotional intelligence provides significant psychological benefits. By understanding and managing emotions, individuals can cultivate greater self-awareness, build stronger relationships, and experience less stress in the workplace. High EQ also contributes to improved mental health, as individuals who are emotionally intelligent are better equipped to handle challenges and maintain emotional balance.

The psychological benefits of emotional intelligence include:

→ **Greater self-awareness**—Understanding one's emotional triggers and responses helps individuals make more informed decisions and avoid reactive behaviors.

→ **Increased empathy**—Being able to empathize with others fosters deeper, more meaningful relationships.

→ **Improved conflict resolution**—Emotional intelligence allows individuals to navigate disagreements with greater ease and find mutually beneficial solutions.

→ **Lower stress levels**—Professionals with high EQ can manage stress more effectively, reducing the impact of workplace pressure on mental health.

→ **Stronger resilience**—Understanding and managing emotions contributes to greater emotional resilience in the face of setbacks and challenges.

BUILDING A CULTURE OF EMOTIONAL INTELLIGENCE IN THE WORKPLACE

Leaders who promote emotional intelligence within their teams help create a supportive and productive culture where people feel respected, valued, and understood. When organizations prioritize emotional intelligence, they encourage self-awareness, empathy, and open communication. These are qualities that improve relationships and support both personal and professional growth. Environments shaped by emotional intelligence foster collaboration, deepen trust among colleagues, and strengthen connections across teams.

In these kinds of cultures, asking for help is seen, not as a weakness, but as a sign of trust and psychological safety. When team members feel safe to admit when they are stuck, unsure, or overwhelmed, it opens the door to real support and shared success. Encouraging people to speak up and seek guidance when needed creates a more resilient and agile team. This kind of team adapts, learns, and grows together. Emotionally intelligent leaders make it clear that no one has to face challenges alone and that support is always available.

As you transition into your professional life, look for workplaces where people are encouraged to share feedback with compassion. Seek environments where leadership models empathy and emotional awareness, and where communication is handled with care and intention. These are the signs of a workplace that values both performance and well-being.

As someone who has developed emotional intelligence through sport by managing stress, reading team dynamics, and responding with poise, you have the tools to shape a workplace culture for the better. When you lead with emotional awareness, you contribute to stronger teams, higher engagement, and a more human, connected workplace.

CORPORATE APPLICATION OF EMOTIONAL INTELLIGENCE
Managing Stress and Maintaining Professionalism

Just as you faced intense moments on the field that tested your mental strength, your professional life will bring its own challenges. Tight deadlines, demanding clients, and high-pressure projects will push your limits. But with strong emotional intelligence, you can manage stress effectively, stay calm when the pressure is on, and maintain the focus needed to reach your goals with confidence and composure.

How athletes apply this:

- ✔ Remaining composed and focused during tense moments, whether it's a game-winning scenario or a critical work deadline.

- ✔ Using relaxation techniques and mental strategies to calm themselves during stressful situations, just as athletes use visualization or breathing exercises to stay focused during competition.

- ✔ Maintaining clarity in decision-making, even when emotions run high, to ensure that work is not compromised by stress or anxiety.

- ✔ Keeping a positive, solution-oriented mindset that helps them maintain productivity and professionalism.

- ✔ Recognizing when they need support and are willing to ask for help.

Understanding and Responding to Coworkers' Emotions Effectively

In sports, your team thrived when you could read your teammates, sense what they needed, and respond with support. The same is true in the workplace. Your emotional intelligence allows you to build stronger relationships by recognizing how others feel and responding with empathy and care. Whether you are offering support during a tough moment, celebrating a teammate's success, or helping someone work through frustration, your ability to understand emotions creates a more connected and supportive work environment.

How athletes apply this:

- Empathizing with teammates when they are facing setbacks or challenges—offering encouragement and support, much like a colleague who understands when a coworker is overwhelmed and provides assistance or reassurance.

- Recognizing when a teammate or coworker is stressed, frustrated, or disengaged and taking the initiative to check in and offer help.

- Using positive communication to express empathy and understanding, fostering an environment where team members feel heard and valued.

- Being aware of body language, tone, and emotional cues to gauge the emotional state of others and respond appropriately.

Building Strong Interpersonal Relationships in the Workplace

High emotional intelligence helps you build strong relationships, which are essential for effective teamwork and leadership. You already know from your time in sports that strong bonds with your teammates were key to success. The same principle applies in your career. When you bring emotional awareness to your workplace, you build trust, resolve conflicts with maturity, and collaborate in ways that strengthen your team. You create an atmosphere where everyone can thrive.

How athletes apply this:

- ✔ Building trust within a team by being supportive, dependable, and emotionally available, much like professionals who create trust with their colleagues through open communication and reliability.

- ✔ Encouraging a positive and inclusive atmosphere, where everyone feels respected and valued, just as athletes cultivate a positive team culture through shared goals and mutual respect.

- ✔ Resolving conflicts and disagreements in a constructive, solution-focused manner, as athletes often have to resolve differences in opinion or strategy to achieve a common goal.

- ✔ Leading by example and fostering team cohesion, both in sports and business, through effective communication and empathy.

📋 Practice Plan

Emotional intelligence is not about suppressing emotions. It is about understanding them, managing them, and using them to stay focused and effective when it matters most. As an athlete, you have already practiced this skill. You stayed calm under pressure, recovered quickly from mistakes, and kept your head in the game when the intensity was high. Those experiences shaped your ability to lead with composure and clarity, making emotional intelligence one of your greatest assets in your professional life.

Use the following questions to reflect on how you've developed emotional intelligence through sport and how it can serve you in your career:

→ When was a time I had to remain calm and composed in a high-pressure moment? What was happening, and how did I stay focused?

→ What mental strategies or techniques did I use to manage stress, nerves, or frustration in training or competition?

→ How did I continue to make clear, smart decisions, even when the stakes were high or emotions were running strong?

→ When did I help keep the mood positive or solution-focused during a difficult moment for my team?

→ What helped me bounce back quickly after a tough loss, mistake, or personal setback?

Now consider how these same skills apply to your future career. In the workplace, you will face pressure, shifting expectations, and emotionally-charged moments just like you did in competition. Ask yourself: How will I respond when a team project starts falling behind or tensions rise in a meeting? What strategies can I use to stay grounded during busy or stressful work weeks? How can I help create a calm, focused environment for others even when things are intense? How will I make sure my emotions support my decision-making rather than distract from it? Your ability to stay steady, focused, and emotionally aware will make you a leader others can trust and a teammate others want to work with. The emotional discipline you built in sport is exactly what helps teams thrive under pressure in business.

Grab a pen—or open a document—and write about how you manage your emotions and mindset. This isn't just about staying in control—it's about showing up at your best when it counts most.

Postgame Recap

Emotional intelligence is a vital skill for both athletes and professionals. Just as you learned to manage your emotions to perform at your best in sport, you must now develop and apply that same emotional intelligence to navigate the challenges of the workplace. When you understand and control your emotions, empathize with others, and build strong relationships, you become a more effective leader, collaborator, and communicator. As you transition from sports to business, emotional intelligence is one of your greatest assets. Your ability to handle stress, connect with others, and foster trust will help you thrive in your career just like it helped you succeed in competition. When you bring the same dedication and focus to your emotional growth as you did to your athletic training, you open the door to greater success, deeper fulfillment, and lasting impact in every area of your life.

10

COMPETITIVE DRIVE AND WORK ETHIC

THE KEYS TO EXCELLENCE

BEHIND THE BENCH

Jamie wasn't driven by approval. They were driven by results. Wins were never enough on its own. If the team played well but they missed key rotations, Jamie was in the gym the next morning. If they scored 18 but gave up an easy basket late, they watched film to fix it. Every game was a checkpoint, not a finish line. Their standard wasn't set by comparison. It was set by what they knew they were capable of. And that made them relentless.

Jamie trained with purpose. Every rep had a reason. If they worked on free throws, it was because they had missed two under pressure. If they ran extra, it was to make sure they never gassed out when it counted. They didn't just practice more. They practiced to solve problems. They tracked performance like a coach. They looked for gaps, and then they closed them. And the minute they reached a goal, they set a new one. Improvement wasn't an event. It was a lifestyle. I never once saw Jamie coast after a win. If anything, they leaned in harder. The question was always, what's next? What's better than this?

That mindset followed them into their professional life. In every role, Jamie became the person people turned to when outcomes mattered. Not because they were loud. Not because they chased credit. But because they delivered. They prepared with precision. They noticed what others missed. And when something worked, they didn't settle in. They asked how to raise the bar again. For Jamie, working hard has never been about looking busy. It has been about getting better, getting sharper, and getting results. Again and again. The scoreboard might say it's over. Jamie is already thinking about the next game.

THE ROLE OF COMPETITIVE DRIVE AND WORK ETHIC IN ATHLETIC SUCCESS

You are driven by an unrelenting desire to be the best. Whether you are striving for a championship title, a personal record, or simply outperforming your competition, you bring a natural competitive spirit that pushes you to go above and beyond. Your drive for excellence is not just about winning. It is about constantly pushing limits, setting higher standards, and seeking continuous improvement. The same competitive fire that fuels your performance in sports is a powerful asset in the corporate world.

You know that success is not achieved by doing the bare minimum. It is built through hard work, persistence, and an unwavering commitment to improvement. You recognize that putting in the extra effort—whether it is another repetition in the gym or extra hours of focused preparation—can make the difference between good and great. This work ethic translates directly to business, where your dedication, initiative, and willingness to go the extra mile set you apart.

Your competitive drive and strong work ethic have helped you push through fatigue, overcome setbacks, and rise to challenges. You already understand that talent alone is not enough. True success requires relentless effort, resilience, and the hunger to improve every single day. That mindset will carry you forward and give you a lasting edge in every professional arena you enter.

Athletes understand:

→ **Excellence requires constant effort.** Achieving greatness isn't about talent alone—it's about continually striving to be better.

→ **Goal-setting is essential.** Athletes set clear, measurable goals for themselves to stay focused and motivated.

→ **Challenges are opportunities.** Every obstacle is a chance to learn, refine skills, and grow stronger.

→ **Resilience is part of the process.** Setbacks are stepping stones to greater success.

→ **Consistency is key.** Work ethic is about showing up every day, even when motivation wanes.

→ **Sacrifices are necessary.** Athletes often give up personal time and comfort to achieve their goals.

These principles do not just make you a great athlete. They make you a great professional. The habits you developed through your dedication to training and improvement translate directly to success in the corporate world. When you apply the same focus, consistency, and effort to your career that you brought to your sport, you position yourself to lead, achieve, and thrive.

HOW COMPETITIVE DRIVE AND WORK ETHIC TRANSLATE TO BUSINESS SUCCESS

"I think goals should never be easy. They should force you to work, even if they are uncomfortable at the time."
— *Michael Phelps*

Michael Phelps didn't just win more Olympic medals than anyone in history—he redefined what it meant to be driven. Behind twenty-three gold medals was a swimmer who trained every single day for five straight years, without missing a session. Not on holidays. Not on his birthday. Not after world records. He didn't chase greatness casually. He committed to it completely.

His training routine was legendary. Two-a-days in the pool. Weightlifting sessions. Calorie-dense diets that fueled six-hour practice days. Film study. Stroke analysis. Recovery protocols. All stacked into a routine that left no margin for laziness. But Phelps didn't view that as sacrifice. He viewed it as the cost of his goals. He once said, *"I wanted to do something no one had ever done before. So I had to do things no one else was willing to do."*

That mentality translated into performance under pressure. In Beijing, London, Rio—when the world was watching—Phelps didn't just win. He delivered moments that seemed scripted: out-touching competitors by hundredths of a second, winning from behind, coming back meet after meet. What looked effortless was actually *the output of years of brutal repetition* and mental rehearsal.

Even after retirement, Phelps carried that same intensity into mental health advocacy, business partnerships, and philanthropy. He became as outspoken about therapy and burnout as he once was about goals and training. And that too required work—different work, but just as intentional. The same drive that pushed him to Olympic podiums now fuels purpose-driven initiatives, all executed with the same obsession for doing things well.

In business, Phelps's example is clear: talent opens the door, but work ethic builds the legacy. If you want to accomplish extraordinary things, you need to build systems around your goals—and then hold yourself to them, relentlessly. Phelps didn't hope to win. He *planned* to win. He reverse-engineered his success from the podium backward—setting incremental benchmarks, tracking his progress, and eliminating anything that didn't serve the mission. Phelps reminds us that the difference between good and legendary isn't usually talent. It's what you're willing to *commit to*—and stay committed to—when it gets uncomfortable.

WHY COMPETITIVE DRIVE AND WORK ETHIC ARE KEY DIFFERENTIATORS IN THE WORKPLACE

In a fast-paced business environment, you rise to the top by showing ambition, drive, and a relentless pursuit of excellence. Employers value people who are self-motivated, goal-oriented, and ready to take on challenges to deliver results. You bring something unique to the workplace because your competitive nature and strong work ethic have been shaped by years of demanding training, discipline, and focus.

Leaders know that athletes know how to:

→ Set ambitious goals
→ Work hard to achieve them
→ Embrace challenges as opportunities for growth

Your competitive drive and work ethic show employers that you bring ambition, focus, and a relentless pursuit of excellence to everything you do. You help create a workplace culture where high performance is expected and challenges are seen as opportunities to grow and prove your potential. This mindset not only sets you apart, it also inspires those around you to raise their own standards.

THE PSYCHOLOGICAL BENEFITS OF COMPETITIVE DRIVE AND WORK ETHIC

Beyond career success, competitive drive and work ethic provide powerful psychological benefits that foster both personal and professional fulfillment. These benefits significantly enhance an individual's well-being, resilience, and overall motivation to achieve success. They help you build a strong sense of purpose and confidence that carries into every challenge you face.

The psychological benefits include:

→ **Increased Resilience**—The desire to succeed helps individuals bounce back quickly from setbacks.

→ **A Growth Mindset**—Challenges are seen as opportunities to learn and improve.

→ **Higher Self-Esteem and Confidence**—Hard work leads to tangible results, boosting self-belief.

→ **Enhanced Motivation**—The drive to succeed fuels continuous improvement and effort.

→ **Sense of Purpose**—Knowing that effort leads to success provides strong direction and motivation.

These psychological benefits do more than support professional success; they also enhance mental well-being. Resilience, a growth mindset, and heightened self-esteem all contribute to your ability to overcome challenges and thrive. With a clear sense of purpose and ongoing motivation, you are better equipped to achieve your goals and maintain fulfillment both in and out of the workplace. These inner strengths help you stay grounded, focused, and energized no matter what obstacles come your way.

BUILDING A CULTURE OF COMPETITIVE DRIVE AND WORK ETHIC IN THE WORKPLACE

Organizations that cultivate a culture of competitive drive and strong work ethic create environments where people are motivated to strive for excellence, take initiative, and push beyond expectations. These cultures thrive when high standards are the norm, achievements are celebrated, and growth is treated as a constant pursuit. In workplaces like this, you will notice that effort is recognized, learning is continuous, and there is a collective mindset of reaching for more.

As an athlete, you bring this energy naturally. You are used to showing up with focus, pushing your limits, and holding yourself to high standards, even when no one is watching. That drive does more than fuel your own success; it raises the bar for the people around you. When you bring your competitive mindset and strong work ethic into the professional world, you help shape a high performance culture, one where excellence becomes contagious and mediocrity has no place.

CORPORATE APPLICATION OF COMPETITIVE DRIVE AND WORK ETHIC
Setting and Achieving Professional Goals

One of the hallmarks of a competitive athlete is your ability to set clear, measurable goals. Whether you were aiming for a championship, improving a specific skill, or setting personal bests, you created a roadmap for success. In the business world, this translates to setting ambitious professional goals. These are goals that challenge you to improve, grow, and excel. When you consistently set and achieve high standards, you not only demonstrate your value but also establish yourself as a key contributor to any organization.

How athletes apply this:

- ✔ Setting SMART (Specific, Measurable, Achievable, Relevant, Time-bound) goals for career advancement.

- ✔ Breaking down long-term professional goals into smaller, actionable steps.

- ✔ Regularly assessing progress and adjusting strategies to stay on track.

- ✔ Working tirelessly to exceed targets, whether in sales numbers, project deliverables, or leadership roles.

126

Taking Initiative and Seeking Career Advancement

Just as you constantly sought ways to improve your performance by refining your technique, training harder, or taking on new challenges, you must now bring that same drive into your professional life. In the corporate world, growth does not happen by waiting. You actively pursue it by expanding your skill set, stepping into leadership roles, and positioning yourself for promotions. Your competitive mindset gives you the edge to keep growing, pushing forward, and standing out.

How athletes apply this:

- Actively seeking new challenges and responsibilities that align with career growth
- Pursuing professional development, such as certifications, workshops, or mentorship.
- Volunteering for challenging projects or leadership roles.
- Seeking feedback and using it to refine techniques or strategies.
- Maintaining a forward-thinking mindset, always striving for the next opportunity.

Continuously Improving Skills and Embracing Challenges

A competitive mindset means never being satisfied with the status quo. It is about always pushing for the next level of excellence. Just as you refined your techniques and analyzed game footage to improve, you now seek every opportunity to enhance your expertise and adapt to new challenges. This mindset keeps you sharp, focused, and ahead of the curve in any professional environment.

How athletes apply this:

- ✔ Committing to lifelong learning and professional development to stay competitive.

- ✔ Welcoming feedback and using it as a tool for refining skills and improving performance.

- ✔ Taking on projects outside their comfort zone to develop new capabilities and expand their expertise.

- ✔ Staying adaptable and embracing change, knowing that flexibility and resilience are key to long-term success.

Demonstrating Persistence and Overcoming Challenges

You often faced adversity in your athletic journey, whether it was injuries, setbacks, or tough losses, but your work ethic kept you moving forward. That same persistence will serve you well in business. Challenges like market shifts, failed projects, or professional disappointments are inevitable, but when you approach them with grit and determination, they become temporary hurdles instead of permanent barriers. Your ability to keep pushing, even when it is hard, is what will set you apart.

How athletes apply this:

- ✔ Developing a mindset that views failure as a learning opportunity rather than a defeat.

- ✔ Rebounding from disappointments by analyzing what went wrong and implementing improvements.

- ✔ Maintaining focus and drive, even in difficult situations, to achieve long-term goals.

- ✔ Building resilience through consistent effort, discipline, and a commitment to growth.

📋 Practice Plan

Your athletic career was built on effort. You showed up, pushed your limits, and found ways to improve even when no one was watching. That competitive drive did more than help you win games. It helped you grow. Now, that same hunger to improve is one of your greatest strengths as a future professional.

This exercise will help you reflect on how your work ethic and internal motivation have shaped your development and how they can fuel your success in the next chapter of your life.

Answer the questions below:

- → When was a time I worked intentionally to grow a specific skill or area of weakness? What was the process, and what kept me committed?

- → How have I used feedback—not just praise, but tough, honest feedback—to improve my performance?

YOUR COMPETITIVE ADVANTAGE

➜ What's an example of a time I pushed outside my comfort zone—by taking on a new role, challenge, or responsibility—and what did I learn?

➜ When did I go above and beyond what was required—on my own initiative—to help my team or better myself?

➜ How did I stay motivated when progress was slow or results didn't come right away?

Work ethic and growth mindset are often what separate those who coast from those who lead. You already know how to grind, learn, and rise to the occasion. The key is bringing that same energy into every room you walk into. Now apply that same drive to your future career. Ask yourself how you will keep growing when there is no coach assigning extra reps. What does it look like to stay competitive and committed in an environment where progress is not always visible? How can you create opportunities to stretch your skills and take ownership of your development? How will you use feedback from managers, coworkers, or results to sharpen your performance and keep improving?

Grab a pen—or open a document—and reflect on what drives you to compete—and how that same drive will carry you forward.

▦ Postgame Recap

Competitive drive and work ethic are key differentiators in both sports and business. As an athlete, your desire to win and constantly improve has been a central motivator throughout

130

your career. In the corporate world, this same competitive spirit fuels goal setting, continuous growth, and the pursuit of excellence. You bring that drive into the workplace by setting ambitious goals, embracing challenges, and continually sharpening your skills.

Your relentless pursuit of excellence does more than elevate your own performance. It raises the standard for your entire team. When you apply your competitive mindset and strong work ethic to your professional life, you set yourself up for long-term success and help drive meaningful results for those around you.

11

ADAPTABILITY AND COACHABILITY

THRIVING IN CHANGING ENVIRONMENTS

BEHIND THE BENCH

Jamie was used to being prepared. They liked structure, game plans, knowing what came next. But during their final season, all of that got tested. The roster changed. Injuries shuffled the lineup. A new assistant coach came in midyear and brought a completely different system. Suddenly, the offense Jamie had mastered was gone. Roles shifted. Timing felt off. The team started slow, and frustration crept in. I could see it in Jamie. They were not just out of rhythm. They were trying to force a version of the game that no longer fit.

What impressed me most was not how they pushed through. It was how they let go.

Jamie did not dig in or complain. They listened. They asked questions. They sat with the new coach and broke down tape, not to defend the old way, but to understand the new one. They helped teammates adjust, adapted their own role, and stayed focused on where the team needed to go next, not where it had been.

Years later, that same mindset became crucial in their first big business challenge.

Jamie had been with their company for just over a year when it was acquired by a larger competitor. Overnight, everything changed. New leadership, new reporting structures, new systems. The uncertainty was thick. People were either defensive or frozen. Some left. Others tried to power through without adjusting. Jamie did what they had learned to do back on the court. They asked better questions. They listened to new leaders without losing sight of what made their team strong. They helped their group translate priorities between cultures, stepped into ambiguity without waiting for instructions, and quietly became a bridge. Between departments, between systems, between people who were not sure what came next.

It was not about knowing every answer. It was about staying open, coachable, and willing to evolve. Adaptability does not mean lowering your standards. It means holding steady to your values while letting go of what no longer fits. Jamie did not just survive the change. They helped others get through it. And in doing so, they became indispensable. Not because they had all the answers, but because they kept learning while everything around them moved.

THE ROLE OF ADAPTABILITY AND COACHABILITY IN ATHLETIC SUCCESS

In the world of sports, nothing ever stays the same. You are constantly faced with changing dynamics, new opponents, unpredictable conditions, injuries, and evolving strategies. Your ability to adapt to these challenges is what sets you apart. What worked last season might not work today, and success depends on your willingness to adjust, grow, and find new ways forward. The same is true in business. Companies must navigate shifting market trends, emerging technologies, organizational changes, and unexpected roadblocks. Your adaptability gives you an edge in this environment.

Just like you once adjusted your strategy mid-game or found a way to overcome a tough loss, you now need to bring that same agility into your career. Adaptability is not just about reacting to change, it is about thriving in it. It is about learning continuously, staying open to new ideas, and seeing every change as a new opportunity. Your ability to stay flexible and maintain a positive mindset when things are uncertain is a trait that will make you stand out in any workplace.

Being coachable is just as important. You have already learned how to listen to feedback, apply it, and grow from it. Whether it came from a coach's advice, a teammate's insight, or your own reflection, you know how to take input and turn it into progress. The same skill is critical in your professional life. When you stay open to learning and embrace constructive criticism, you position yourself for consistent growth and long-term success.

In sports, your willingness to adapt and be coached helped you stay competitive. You shifted your game plan when conditions changed. You pushed yourself to adjust when strategies fell short. You stayed ready, open, and responsive. Those same habits will serve you now. Adaptability and coachability are not just survival skills—they are leadership qualities. And you already have them.

Athletes understand:

→ **Success requires flexibility**—The ability to change course mid-game can be the difference between victory and defeat.

→ **Challenges are opportunities to innovate**—When something unexpected occurs, athletes often need to come up with creative solutions and new approaches.

→ **Adaptation is a constant process**—Athletes are always adjusting to improve performance, whether it's tweaking their training regimen, adjusting tactics, or recovering from injuries.

→ **Mental toughness is essential**—Accepting change with a positive mindset and staying focused on the bigger picture is what helps athletes adapt successfully.

→ **Coachability drives improvement**—Athletes understand that being open to feedback and applying it leads to better performance and greater success.

The same adaptability and coachability that athletes develop in response to unpredictable sports conditions are essential in the professional world, where market trends,

YOUR COMPETITIVE ADVANTAGE

organizational shifts, and personal career paths can evolve rapidly. When you stay open to change and willing to learn, you position yourself to grow through any challenge instead of being held back by it. Your ability to adjust, improve, and move forward with confidence is what will set you apart in every stage of your career.

HOW ADAPTABILITY AND COACHABILITY TRANSLATE TO BUSINESS SUCCESS

"You're always going to have to work harder, dig deeper, and prove yourself. And if you're not willing to learn, you'll fall behind."

— *Lindsey Vonn*

Alpine skiing is a sport that demands precision, guts, and above all, adaptability. No two runs are ever the same. The snow shifts. The wind picks up. The course changes by the hour. Lindsey Vonn mastered not just the physical challenge of flying down a mountain at 80 miles per hour, but also the mental agility required to adjust, recalibrate, and perform under pressure. Her greatness was built on more than strength and speed. It was grounded in coachability. She approached every feedback session with humility, studying film like it was a playbook and welcoming critique from coaches and technicians alike. Most importantly, she never flinched at hard truths. If a coach told her she was too aggressive in a turn or too hesitant off the start, she didn't push back. She processed the feedback, made changes, and came back sharper. Her ability to absorb constructive criticism without becoming defensive, and to let it sharpen rather than shrink her, is what kept her evolving while others plateaued. Her agility was not just physical. It was intellectual. It was emotional. And it was relentless.

That same combination of coachability and agility became the engine behind Vonn's success after skiing. In business, she did not rely on her résumé. She chose to lead by learning. Whether launching the Lindsey Vonn Foundation or investing in performance-focused brands like YNIQ, she sought out advisors, asked sharp questions, and invited feedback even when it was difficult to hear. She has been candid about the fact that some of her biggest growth came when people were honest about what she didn't yet know. Instead of seeing that as criticism, she saw it as clarity. Vonn understands that the terrain of business, like snow, is always shifting. Staying relevant requires the courage to pivot and the humility to be coached. She is building her second act with the same principle that defined her first. A willingness to be shaped by others, and the agility to transform that input into forward motion. That is what makes her dangerous in sport, in business, and in whatever mountain she chooses to climb next.

WHY ADAPTABILITY AND COACHABILITY ARE KEY DIFFERENTIATORS IN THE WORKPLACE

In today's business world, where technological advancements and market conditions are in constant flux, adaptability and

YOUR COMPETITIVE ADVANTAGE

coachability are more valuable than ever. Employees who can navigate changes with ease, learn new skills quickly, and stay productive during transitions are highly sought after by employers. Adaptability demonstrates resilience, creativity, and a commitment to continuous improvement, while coachability signals a willingness to learn and improve based on feedback. Both are essential for success in a dynamic business environment, and they help you grow into a professional who thrives no matter what challenges arise.

For employers, an athlete brings:

→ Openness
→ Flexibility
→ Motivation to grow and develop

For employers, adaptable and coachable employees are seen as problem solvers, innovators, and leaders. They are the individuals who can handle the unknown and turn challenges into opportunities. Adaptability allows you to remain effective even when circumstances change unexpectedly, while coachability ensures that you continuously evolve to meet the demands of your role. These qualities not only help you stand out but also make you someone your team can rely on in any situation.

THE PSYCHOLOGICAL BENEFITS OF ADAPTABILITY AND COACHABILITY

Adaptability and coachability are critical skills in both personal and professional life, offering valuable psychological benefits that help you navigate change and uncertainty with ease. These strengths build your mental resilience and contribute to your ongoing growth. When you are adaptable and coachable, you embrace change, stay calm under pressure, and maintain a positive mindset. This approach not only helps you overcome challenges but also boosts your confidence and equips you to thrive in any environment.

The psychological benefits of adaptability and coachability include:

→ **Increased Resilience**—Adaptable individuals are better equipped to handle stress and bounce back from challenges.

→ **Enhanced Problem-Solving Skills**—They approach challenges from multiple perspectives, finding creative solutions.

→ **Greater Emotional Stability**—Adaptable individuals maintain a positive outlook, even in uncertain situations.

→ **Higher Confidence**—Being comfortable in unfamiliar environments boosts their belief in their ability to succeed.

→ **Improved Learning and Growth**—Coachable individuals continually evolve, applying feedback to develop new skills and refine their abilities.

These psychological benefits help you thrive in dynamic environments, effectively manage stress, and remain calm in the face of adversity. Your ability to embrace change and learn from feedback not only enhances your problem-solving capacity but also strengthens your emotional resilience and overall self-assurance. These traits allow you to stay steady under pressure and continue growing no matter what challenges come your way.

BUILDING A CULTURE OF ADAPTABILITY AND COACHABILITY IN THE WORKPLACE

Organizations that foster adaptability and coachability create environments where people feel encouraged to embrace change, try new things, and grow through experience. These workplaces promote ongoing learning, open feedback, and a mindset that views change as a chance to improve rather than something to fear. In cultures like this, you will see teams that learn together, stay flexible, and push forward even when the path ahead is uncertain.

As someone who has already adapted to new roles, responded to feedback, and embraced tough challenges in sport, you are well prepared to bring this mindset into your professional life. Your ability to pivot with confidence, learn quickly, and remain open to growth makes you an invaluable part of any team. When you carry your adaptability and coachability into the workplace, you help shape a culture that thrives in motion and always looks ahead to what is possible.

CORPORATE APPLICATION OF DISCIPLINE
Quickly Adjusting to New Company Policies or Technologies

Just as you adjusted to new strategies or playing conditions in your athletic career, you must now be ready to learn new policies, systems, or technologies that impact your work. Embracing these changes without hesitation allows you to stay effective and perform at a high level. When you can navigate shifting workplace expectations or technological advancements with ease, you become a valuable asset to any organization. Your ability to adapt quickly and continue delivering results sets you apart in a fast-moving professional world.

How athletes apply this:

✔ Staying current with new tools, systems, or platforms used in the workplace.

✔ Quickly learning new software or adapting to new organizational processes.

✔ Embracing changes in job responsibilities or company direction without resistance.

✔ Keeping a positive attitude in the face of new challenges, as they would in adjusting to a change in strategy or team dynamics.

Remaining Flexible and Open to New Roles and Responsibilities

You were often asked to take on new positions, roles, or responsibilities depending on what your team needed. Maybe you switched positions or stepped up when a teammate was injured. You understood the importance of being flexible and doing what was best for the group. That same mindset will serve you well in the business world. When you stay open to new roles, cross-department collaboration, or leadership opportunities, you show that you are adaptable and proactive. Your willingness to take on new challenges and build new skills can set you apart and accelerate your growth in any professional environment.

How athletes apply this:

- ✔ Volunteering for new projects or taking on new challenges outside of their usual role.

- ✔ Demonstrating a willingness to learn and take on unfamiliar tasks or responsibilities.

- ✔ Collaborating with others in different departments or teams to meet the company's needs.

- ✔ Adjusting personal career goals and priorities based on shifting organizational objectives.

Thriving in Fast-Paced and Evolving Business Environments

Just as you had to stay focused and perform at your best when the game was on the line, you now need to bring that same level of focus and resilience into your career. In sports, unexpected weather, a tough opponent, or a loud crowd could change everything in a moment. In business, shifting market trends, economic conditions, and evolving customer needs can do the same. But you already know how to adjust without losing your edge. Your ability to stay composed, adapt quickly, and keep delivering in high-pressure situations will help you thrive in any fast-changing professional environment.

How athletes apply this:

- ✔ Managing stress and staying calm during periods of rapid change or uncertainty.

- ✔ Quickly assessing new situations and adjusting plans or strategies accordingly.

- ✔ Remaining productive and focused during times of transition, such as organizational restructuring or the introduction of new technology.

- ✔ Embracing fast-paced environments and using their competitive drive to stay ahead of changing circumstances.

Practice Plan

In sport, plans change. Lineups shift. Roles evolve. And if you want to succeed, you learn to adjust quickly. Whether you were thrown into a new position midseason, asked to fill in for an injured teammate, or needed to learn something fast, you have already shown what it means to be adaptable and coachable. Those same traits are essential in the workplace, where businesses change, roles shift, and flexibility becomes a key advantage. Your ability to stay composed, embrace feedback, and pivot with confidence is not just an asset. It is a skill that will continue to set you apart in every professional setting.

Use the questions below to reflect on moments when you had to stay open, flexible, and ready to learn something new:

→ When did I take on responsibilities outside of my normal role or comfort zone? How did I handle that shift, and what was the result?

→ How have I responded when asked to adjust my goals or priorities based on the team's or organization's needs?

→ What's an example of a time I collaborated with people from different roles, skill sets, or personalities to get something done?

→ When have I taken feedback or direction and quickly applied it to improve or pivot?

→ When was a time I had to do something I'd never done before? How did I approach the challenge, and what helped me succeed?

Being adaptable does not mean having no direction. It means being steady in motion, capable of learning, adjusting, and contributing wherever you are needed. And being coachable is not about always being told what to do. It is about showing that you are open to growth and humble enough to keep learning, no matter where you start.

Now look ahead to your career. Ask yourself: How will I stay flexible when my job evolves or expectations change? What mindset will I bring to new tasks, teams, or industries I have not worked in before? How can I show others that I am open to learning, even when I do not have all the answers yet? How will I continue to seek growth and development, even in unfamiliar or uncomfortable situations?

Grab a pen—or open a document—and reflect on how you've adapted, and how that mindset will help you thrive in your next chapter.

Postgame Recap

Adaptability and coachability are crucial skills for your success both as an athlete and as a professional. Just as you had to adjust your strategies, recover from injuries, and adapt to changing conditions on the field, you now need to navigate shifting market trends, organizational changes, and new technologies in the workplace.

When you embrace change, stay flexible, and learn continuously from feedback, you put yourself in a position to thrive in fast-paced and dynamic environments. Your ability to stay calm under pressure, respond quickly to new

145

situations, and find creative solutions to challenges makes you an invaluable contributor to any organization. As the business world continues to evolve, these traits will be what set you apart and keep you growing.

12

RESILIENCE

BEHIND THE BENCH

E very athlete hits a wall. For Jamie, it came in the middle of their sophomore year. A stress fracture in their foot sidelined them just as the season was hitting its stride. They had been starting, finding rhythm, growing into a leadership role. And just like that, it was all paused. What made it worse was not just the injury. It was the stillness. While the team traveled and played, Jamie stayed behind. While practices buzzed, they were in rehab, doing small, repetitive exercises in a quiet room. Progress was slow. Pain flared. Setbacks came out of nowhere. They had always outworked problems. But now, effort was not enough. They had to wait. They had to recover. They had to be patient. That was the test.

I remember checking in with them during that stretch. They did not complain. But they did not pretend to be fine either. They were honest about the frustration. And then, little by little, they shifted their focus. Not to what they could not do, but to what they could. Jamie watched film. They studied the game from the sideline. They cheered teammates. They strengthened other parts of their body. They found ways to contribute even while sitting out. And when they came back, they were different. Not just physically. Mentally. Their perspective had changed. They did not just play with urgency. They played with appreciation. Every drill mattered more. Every moment on the court felt earned. They had gone through something hard, and they had not let it harden them. It had sharpened them.

Years later, I watched them navigate another wall. A business pitch that fell through after months of work. A restructuring that dissolved a team they had built. Setbacks that would rattle anyone. But Jamie stayed steady. They adjusted, regrouped, and got back to work. Not with false optimism, but with perspective. They had learned how to move through hard things without losing who they were. That is resilience. Not just endurance, but growth through adversity. Jamie had every reason to shut down. Instead, they built themselves back up and helped others do the same.

THE ROLE OF RESILIENCE IN ATHLETIC SUCCESS

Resilience is the silent force that drives success, both on the field and in your future career. In sport, resilience is your ability to recover from setbacks, learn from failure, and keep pushing forward in the face of adversity. Whether it was a heartbreaking loss, a tough injury, or a stretch of poor performance, you learned to develop the mental toughness needed to overcome challenges and stay focused on your goals.

In the professional world, resilience shows up in how you handle rejection, adjust to new circumstances, and stay committed even when progress is slow or obstacles appear. Employers value resilience because it reflects your capacity to handle adversity, stay steady under pressure, and remain motivated when things get hard.

This is exactly what you have trained for. In sport, failure was never final. It was your chance to grow and get better. The same is true in business. Resilience helps you bounce back stronger and use your experiences to adapt, lead, and achieve more. Your ability to stay persistent, even when the path gets tough, is one of your greatest advantages as you step into a new environment.

Resilience has always been a part of your journey. You have worked through losses, injuries, and setbacks with grit and determination. Resilience does not just mean getting back up. It means learning from every stumble, changing your approach, and improving every time. In sport, you knew that every challenge held a lesson. Carry that mindset forward. Embrace adversity as the fuel for growth and the proof of your strength.

Athletes understand:

→ **Failure is temporary**—Losses and mistakes don't define an athlete's future success; it's the ability to recover and learn from them that matters.

→ **Adversity builds strength**—Difficult times—whether physical or mental—forge resilience and prepare athletes for greater challenges.

→ **The mental game is just as important as the physical one**— Resilience helps athletes remain focused, confident, and motivated, even in high-pressure situations.

→ **Growth comes from setbacks**—The best athletes learn from their failures, using them as stepping stones to improvement.

→ **Patience and persistence are key**—Resilient athletes understand that success is a marathon, not a sprint.

These qualities of resilience are not just about bouncing back physically. They reflect the mental and emotional endurance that allows you to persist through the toughest moments. It is the mindset that keeps you moving forward, even when progress feels slow and the challenges seem overwhelming. This same resilience becomes one of your greatest strengths in the corporate world, where persistence, focus, and inner toughness are essential to achieving success.

HOW RESILIENCE TRANSLATES TO BUSINESS SUCCESS

"I'm really thankful for adversity. I think it makes me a stronger person."

— *Simone Biles*

Simone Biles was already the most decorated gymnast in history when she made what many considered an unthinkable decision: she stepped away—from the Olympics, from the spotlight, from the expectation to be superhuman. But that moment didn't reveal weakness. It revealed *resilience*—the kind that comes not from pushing harder, but from knowing when to protect what matters most.

For years, Biles performed under extraordinary pressure. She carried the weight of a sport, a nation, and a legacy. She competed with precision, grace, and power unmatched in modern gymnastics. But behind the scenes, she was navigating a storm: public trauma, personal grief, physical injuries, and mental exhaustion. In Tokyo, it all converged. She pulled herself out of multiple events—not because she couldn't compete, but because doing so would have risked her health and safety.

And then something remarkable happened: she came back. Not for medals, not for redemption, but to finish on *her* terms. She returned for the balance beam, performed a stripped-down routine, and won bronze. But more importantly, she modeled a different kind of resilience— one rooted in boundaries, self-awareness, and the courage to prioritize recovery over reputation.

Off the mat, Biles has become a mental health advocate, entrepreneur, and role model for sustainable excellence. She's launched her own gymnastics tour, partnered with wellness and financial brands, and spoken openly about what it means to perform under pressure in every area of life. Her ability to move forward—not by pretending she was unaffected, but by rebuilding slowly and intentionally—is the exact mindset required in business and leadership.

In high-performance organizations, resilience is often misunderstood. It's praised as the ability to "power through," to absorb pressure without breaking. But the most effective professionals know something deeper: *resilience is about sustainability*. It's about protecting your ability to perform tomorrow—not just surviving today.

Biles's approach translates directly into business culture. It's about knowing when to reset to prevent burnout. About giving your team permission to pause and rethink—not just plow forward. It's creating environments where people don't have to break in order to be taken seriously. Her example challenges outdated models of leadership and shows that the strongest organizations aren't the ones that never wobble. They're the ones that know how to *re-center* when they do.

Simone Biles reminds us: real strength doesn't always look like pushing through. Sometimes, it looks like pausing, realigning, and rising again—on your own terms, with your values intact.

WHY RESILIENCE IS A KEY DIFFERENTIATOR IN THE WORKPLACE

In any profession, setbacks are unavoidable. What sets you apart as a top performer is your ability to handle adversity with grace and determination. In the business world, your resilience shows that you can stay productive, creative, and motivated, even when things do not go according to plan. When you stay focused on your long-term goals and keep pushing forward despite challenges, you show others that you are reliable, persistent, and committed to excellence.

Employers know that athletes have the ability to:

→ Learn from experience
→ Bounce back from setbacks
→ Stay focused on long-term goals

You are highly resilient because of the challenges you have faced in sport. Whether you came back from an injury, fought through a losing streak, or pushed through mental fatigue, you built the mental toughness needed to persevere. Your ability to stay composed under pressure and stay focused on the bigger picture makes you a valuable asset in any workplace.

Resilience also builds leadership. When you have overcome adversity yourself, you are uniquely equipped to guide others through tough moments. You naturally inspire your teammates, lead by example, and help those around you keep moving forward no matter the circumstances.

THE PSYCHOLOGICAL BENEFITS OF RESILIENCE

Beyond career success, resilience gives you powerful psychological advantages that support both personal and professional fulfillment. When you are resilient, you build emotional stability, strengthen your confidence, and develop a growth mindset. You become better equipped to manage stress, regulate your emotions, and recover from setbacks. Resilience reminds you that challenges are a natural part of life. Instead of letting them defeat you, you use them to grow stronger and sharpen your mental toughness. The strength you build through resilience keeps you moving forward, focused on your goals, and confident in your ability to overcome whatever stands in your way.

The psychological benefits of resilience include:

→ **Increased motivation**—Resilient individuals maintain their drive even when facing failure or adversity.

→ **Better stress management**—They stay calm and focused during high-pressure situations.

→ **Stronger self-confidence**—Overcoming challenges and learning from mistakes builds self-assurance.

→ **Improved decision-making**—They remain clear-headed under pressure, particularly when the stakes are high.

→ **Long-term focus**—Resilient individuals prioritize persistence over comfort, remaining committed to growth even when faced with difficulties.

BUILDING A CULTURE OF RESILIENCE IN THE WORKPLACE

Organizations that value resilience create environments where growth, innovation, and perseverance are part of the daily rhythm. In these workplaces, challenges are seen as opportunities to improve, and setbacks are viewed as part of the journey. Employees are supported with the tools and encouragement they need to develop mental strength, take risks, and bounce back stronger. When people feel safe to fail forward, they become more willing to stretch themselves and take on meaningful goals.

You have already built this resilience through your athletic career. You know what it feels like to fall short, regroup, and come back better. When you bring that mindset into the workplace, you help build a culture where determination and persistence are celebrated. You can be a leader who helps others push through hard moments, stay focused under pressure, and continue to grow—no matter what comes next.

CORPORATE APPLICATION OF RESILIENCE
Handling Constructive Criticism and Using It to Improve

Just as you faced critique from your coaches, you will receive feedback from colleagues, managers, and clients in your professional life. Resilience means you do not take that feedback personally. You see it as a valuable opportunity to grow. When you are resilient, you listen, reflect, and use what you learn to get better. You take ownership of your development and use every bit of feedback to sharpen your performance and strengthen your impact.

How athletes apply this:

- ✔ Viewing feedback as a tool for self-improvement, rather than as a negative judgment.

- ✔ Continuously seeking ways to enhance performance based on constructive criticism.

- ✔ Demonstrating a willingness to adjust strategies and methods in the face of feedback.

Navigating Setbacks and Rejection

Challenges will arise in your professional life just like they did during unexpected losses or periods of injury in your athletic career. You might deal with rejected proposals, failed projects, or goals that fall short. Resilience helps you stay focused on the bigger picture instead of getting stuck in short-term disappointments. You learn to view these setbacks as opportunities to pivot, adapt, and return even stronger.

How athletes apply this:

- ✔ Treating rejection or failure as part of the learning process, rather than a permanent defeat.

- ✔ Adjusting strategies and goals in response to setbacks.

- ✔ Using each failure as motivation to push harder and refine skills.

Staying Confident and Persistent Under Pressure

In both sports and business, high-pressure situations are inevitable. Whether it is a final championship game or a crucial presentation, you need to remain calm, composed, and confident under stress. Your resilience helps you stay persistent, even when the pressure is intense. It gives you the strength to perform at your best when it matters most and to keep moving forward no matter the obstacles in your way.

How athletes apply this:

- ✔ Keeping a positive mindset, even when the odds are stacked against them.

- ✔ Maintaining focus on goals, regardless of immediate setbacks.

- ✔ Using pressure as a motivator to perform at their best, rather than as a barrier to success.

📋 Practice Plan

Resilience is the ability to recover, reset, and refocus when things do not go as planned. As an athlete, you have faced adversity through missed plays, tough losses, injuries, or moments when you were not in the starting lineup. And yet, you kept showing up. You learned how to take feedback, even when it was difficult to hear, and use it as fuel for improvement. That mindset is exactly what will help you succeed in whatever career path you choose.

Use the following questions to reflect on your ability to bounce back, stay focused, and grow through difficulty:

→ When was a time I experienced failure, disappointment, or a setback in sport? What happened, and how did I respond?

→ How have I handled feedback or criticism—especially when it wasn't delivered well? What helped me stay open to the message instead of taking it personally?

→ When did I treat rejection as a learning opportunity instead of a defeat? How did I use that moment to grow stronger or refine my skills?

→ What strategies or habits helped me stay motivated during difficult seasons or personal struggles?

→ How have I adjusted my approach, goals, or mindset after a setback to come back better prepared?

Resilience means treating failure as feedback—not as a reason to stop but as a call to grow. You have already shown that you can handle hard moments in sport. Now it is time to bring that same strength into your next challenge. Start applying this mindset to your career. Ask yourself: How will I respond when something does not go my way at work, whether it is a missed promotion, a tough review, or an unsuccessful project? What tools can I use to stay grounded and focused on long-term growth? How will I turn future setbacks into fuel and not to hold me back, but to drive me forward? How can I stay confident while remaining open to growth, reflection, and course correction?

Grab a pen—or open a document—and reflect on what's made you resilient—and how that resilience will carry you forward.

Postgame Recap

Resilience is the key to overcoming challenges, both in sports and business. The ability to bounce back from setbacks, learn from failure, and maintain a positive, focused mindset is what drives long-term success. As an athlete transitioning into the workforce, resilience is already part of your mindset. The next step is applying that mental toughness to your professional environment so you can rise above the challenges that come your way in business.

You already have the resilience needed to thrive in any industry. With the right perspective, you can turn adversity into opportunity, pushing forward and achieving success even in the face of obstacles. Just like in sports, the journey to success in business is rarely linear. Resilience is what keeps you moving forward no matter what.

13

BRINGING IT ALL TOGETHER

You have reached the final chapter of your journey. At this point, you have explored every major skill that sets you apart as an athlete and will continue to define you as a professional. You have learned what each skill looks like in action, what it means in high-pressure environments, and how it shapes leadership, teamwork, and personal growth.

In each chapter, you worked through the Practice Plan section. You reflected on how you demonstrated discipline, resilience, leadership, teamwork, time management, competitive drive, adaptability, communication, work ethic, and emotional intelligence. You thought about your own experiences and how those moments built your identity. That process helped you understand who you are and what you bring to the table. All of those thoughts, examples, and notes you captured in your Career Playbook were designed for this moment. That section is your organized record of everything you've learned about yourself.

Now it is time to take the next step. This chapter is about turning reflection into action. It is where you use what you know to move forward with confidence. Everything you wrote, remembered, and uncovered through the Practice Plans becomes the foundation for your resume, your interviews, your career planning, and your daily habits. Go back to your Career Playbook now and use it as the starting point for what comes next. Those notes will help you pull real stories, clear strengths, and specific examples that strengthen your resume and elevate your interview skills.

You are not starting from zero. You are starting from strength. You are not guessing your way forward. You are using real experiences and proven qualities to guide your next move.

This is the moment to bring it all together and put it into practice. Let's get started.

THE RESUME: SHOWCASING YOUR GAME-CHANGING SKILLS TO EMPLOYERS

Your next challenge is to clearly communicate your strengths to employers. Both your resume and your interview responses are snapshots of who you are. Make sure they reflect the discipline, resilience, and leadership you developed through sport. Every bullet point on your resume and every interview answer is an opportunity to show how your athletic background sets you apart.

KEEP IT SIMPLE AND POLISHED

→ Limit it to one page

→ Use a clean layout with clear headings and bullet points

→ Avoid sports jargon; use universal business language

→ Use strong, active verbs like "led," "organized," "achieved," and "managed"

→ Focus on measurable accomplishments

→ Align your strengths with the job you want

→ Emphasize transferable skills that apply to the professional world

KEY RESUME SECTIONS WITH EXAMPLES

→ **Contact Information:** Place this at the very top and make it easy to read:

  ▷ Full Name
  ▷ Phone Number
  ▷ Professional Email Address
  ▷ LinkedIn Profile (optional but recommended)
  ▷ City and State (no need for full address)

➜ **Professional Summary:** Write 2–3 lines at the top that summarize who you are, your goals, and what you bring to the table. Your summary should highlight your athletic background and your readiness for the next chapter.

   ▷ *Example: "Disciplined and driven former collegiate athlete transitioning into business with proven skills in leadership, time management, and teamwork. Eager to bring a competitive mindset and results-oriented focus to a growth-focused organization."*

   ▷ *Example: "Former Division I athlete with a competitive mindset, proven leadership experience, and a strong academic foundation in business. Eager to apply my discipline and communication skills to a dynamic, team-driven company."*

➜ **Experience:** You've already mastered performing under pressure, working in diverse teams, setting and achieving ambitious goals, leading peers, and staying accountable and coachable. Even part-time jobs, summer internships, or seasonal roles demonstrate responsibility, consistency, and a strong work ethic. Use all relevant experience; include leadership roles, volunteer coaching, and internships. These experiences round out your story and show your initiative beyond the field. These provide proof of your readiness for business challenges.

→ **Use Action Verbs and Metrics:** Highlight achievements with language that emphasizes outcomes. Numbers stand out. Quantify your impact. Numbers give credibility and clarity. Say things like:

▷ *Example:* "Led offseason workouts, improving team accountability and reducing tardiness by 30 percent."

▷ *Example:* "Organized film sessions to analyze opponent strategies, leading to a 20 percent improvement in game-day execution."

▷ *Example:* "Managed team travel logistics for 15 athletes across multiple events."

▷ *Example:* "Balanced 20+ hours of weekly training while maintaining Dean's List status."

→ **Showcase Transferable Skills:** Use direct, results-oriented language that connects your experience to business outcomes. For example:

▷ *Discipline example:* "Maintained peak athletic performance while balancing full academic course load, consistently meeting deadlines."

▷ *Leadership example:* "Served as team captain, leading strategy sessions and mentoring underclassmen."

▷ *Time Management example:* "Effectively managed daily training, travel, and academics, graduating with a 3.8 GPA."

→ **Include Internships, Campus Roles, or Volunteer Work:**
If you were part of the Student-Athlete Advisory
Committee, academic clubs, or volunteer programs,
highlight it here. These experiences prove your
readiness to learn and grow in professional settings.

  ▷ *Example: "Marketing Intern—Assisted with campaign
  research and social media content planning."*

  ▷ *Example: "Student-Athlete Advisory Committee—
  Represented team in monthly leadership meetings
  and served as liaison between coaching staff and
  student-athletes to improve team experience."*

→ **Include Athletic Experience as a Key Section:** Don't
bury your sports experience. Use it to showcase
leadership, dedication, and performance:

  ▷ *Example: "Team Captain, Women's Soccer | 2021–
  2024—Led team to two conference titles. Facilitated
  communication between coaches and players."*

  ▷ *Example: "Men's Basketball Leader | 2021–2024—
  Mentored younger athletes and led team through
  high-pressure situations, including two conference
  championship appearances."*

→ **Tailor each resume to the Role:** Customize your
resume for each job you apply to. Many companies
now use Applicant Tracking Systems (ATS) which is
software powered by Artificial Intelligence (AI), to
screen resumes before a human ever sees them. These

systems scan for keywords and phrases that match the job description. If your resume doesn't reflect the language in the posting, it might get filtered out, even if you're qualified. Tailoring doesn't mean making your resume longer. It means making it more precise and aligned with the role. Start by reading the job description closely. Look for the top skills, traits, and qualifications the employer highlights. Then show how your background, especially your athletic experience, demonstrates those same strengths.

▷ *Example: If you're applying for a **leadership** role, emphasize your time as a team captain, your ability to motivate others, make strategic decisions, and create a winning culture.*

▷ *Example: If a job emphasizes **teamwork**, highlight how you contributed to team culture, supported others, and achieved shared goals under pressure.*

▷ *Example: If they ask for **data analysis** or **technical skills**, mention your experience with stats, film breakdowns, performance tracking apps, or wearable technology.*

▷ *Example: For **client-facing** roles, underscore your communication, emotional intelligence, and adaptability—skills sharpened by representing your team and adjusting to dynamic environments.*

→ **Skills:** Your skills section should reflect your business readiness. Highlight both soft skills that drive workplace performance and hard skills that show technical competence. This can be a list and usually on the left or right side of the resume. A vertical list in a sidebar keeps your skills visible at a glance, separate from the main body of experience and education. Avoid overloading this section. Keep it concise and relevant to the job you are applying for. Prioritize skills mentioned in the job description. Here are some examples:

▷ *Soft skills:* Leadership, time management, adaptability, resilience

▷ *Hard skills:* Microsoft Office, Excel, Google Workspace, social media management, Salesforce, film and data analysis tools

→ **Education:** Your education section is more than just where you went to school—it's a chance to highlight academic achievement, discipline, and how you balanced school with your athletic commitments. Employers respect candidates who succeed both on the field and in the classroom. Include:

▷ Full name of your school
▷ Degree (completed or in progress)
▷ Major and minor (if applicable)
▷ Graduation year or expected graduation date
▷ Awards or Honors, GPA (if 3.5 or higher)
▷ Sport and years of participation

▷ *Example:*

University of Connecticut
Bachelor of Arts in Communications, Minor
in Business
Expected Graduation: May 2025
GPA: 3.7
Dean's List, 6 semesters
NCAA Division I Student-Athlete, Women's
Soccer (2021–2025)
Relevant Coursework: Marketing Principles,
Organizational Behavior
Capstone Project on Performance Mindset in
High-Pressure Situations

THE INTERVIEW: SHOWCASING YOUR COMPETITIVE EDGE IN CONVERSATION

When you step into an interview, you bring more than your resume—you bring experiences, lessons, and a competitive mindset. Use your athletic background to tell powerful, results-driven stories that connect directly to the role you're pursuing.

Use the STAR Method

Structure your responses with **Situation**, **Task**, **Action**, and **Result**. Make your experiences easy to follow and rich with meaning. Many companies use structured, behavioral interview questions. This means they are looking to learn more than what you did, but how you did it.

Prepare for questions such as:

→ Tell me about a time when you had to resolve conflict
→ Tell me about a time when you made a mistake and learned from it
→ Tell me about a time when you had to adapt quickly
→ Tell me about a time when you motivated a teammate or group

  ▷ *Example:*
  Q: *Tell me about a time you had to show leadership.*
  A: *"As team captain, I led my team through a losing streak mid-season. I organized extra film sessions, encouraged open conversations, and helped rebuild our confidence. We ended the season on a five-game winning streak and made the playoffs."*

Highlight Resilience and Adaptability

Employers value candidates who can bounce back and adjust in fast-changing environments. Use athletic examples to show your mental toughness.

  ▷ *Example: "After a season-ending injury, I focused on rehab, supported my team from the sidelines, and returned the next year to earn All-Conference honors."*

  ▷ *Example: "I switched from offense to defense mid-season and spent extra hours studying film to learn the new system. By the end of the season, I was starting in a playoff game."*

> ▷ *Example: "When a new coach joined the program, I adapted to a different style of leadership and helped my teammates adjust to new expectations."*

Demonstrate Emotional Intelligence

Share moments where you supported a struggling teammate, diffused conflict, or led during crisis. Show you understand people as well as problems.

> ▷ *Example: "I noticed a freshman struggling with confidence after a tough game, so I pulled them aside, shared my own early struggles, and encouraged them to keep pushing. That player went on to score the winning goal the following week."*

> ▷ *Example: "During a tense moment in practice, I stepped in to calm a conflict between teammates and redirected our focus to the common goal."*

> ▷ *Example: "As a leader, I learned to recognize when teammates were burning out and worked with coaches to adjust workloads and keep morale high."*

Be Confident and Humble

Own your strengths, but credit your team and recognize your growth areas. Employers appreciate both confidence and coachability. Show you are proud of your work, but still hungry to learn. Talk about your achievements with pride, but be humble. Acknowledge your teammates, coaches, and mentors. Reflect on how feedback helped you improve.

> ▷ *Example: "I'm proud of my leadership role, but I always tried to credit my teammates. I also learned to accept feedback quickly, which helped me develop into a more effective communicator."*

Ask Great Questions

Just like you asked your coach how to get better, ask your interviewer thoughtful questions about the company, culture, or team dynamics. It shows maturity and strategic thinking.

> ▷ *Example: "How does your team define success in this role?"*

> ▷ *Example: "What are the biggest challenges your team is facing right now?"*

> ▷ *Example: "What kind of feedback and support can I expect in this position?"*

> ▷ *Example: "Can you please describe the culture here and what makes someone thrive in it?"*

Prepare, Then Perform

Treat the interview like a game. Study your opponent (the company), know your plays (your stories), and go in confident. Just like on the field, preparation leads to peak performance

RESOURCES FOR YOUR CAREER TRANSITION

Transitioning from an athletic career to the corporate world can be challenging, but there are numerous resources available to help you make the leap successfully. This appendix includes networking tips, online courses, certifications, and professional organizations that can support you as you embark on your new career path.

Networking Tips

Building a professional network is one of the most valuable steps you can take during your career transition. As an athlete, you're accustomed to working as part of a team, and networking in the corporate world is no different. Here are some tips to help you expand your network and make meaningful connections:

→ **Leverage your alumni network:** Reach out to your college or university's alumni network, especially those who have transitioned from sports into successful careers. They can offer advice, mentorship, and potential job leads.

→ **Attend industry events:** Conferences, trade shows, and networking events are great opportunities to meet professionals in your field. Look for events related to your desired industry, even if they are virtual.

→ **Use LinkedIn effectively:** Create a polished LinkedIn profile that highlights your transferable skills. Connect with professionals in your desired field and engage in relevant discussions or post content showcasing your insights and expertise.

→ **Informational interviews:** Take the initiative to schedule informational interviews with professionals in roles you're interested in. This can help you learn about the industry, build connections, and potentially uncover hidden job opportunities.

→ **Find a mentor:** Seek out mentors who can guide you through the transition process. Mentors can be individuals who have successfully made the switch from sports to business or seasoned professionals in your target industry.

Online Courses and Certifications

As you transition into the workforce, further education and skill development can give you an edge in the job market. Below are some online courses and certifications that can help you enhance your qualifications and develop skills relevant to your career:

→ **LinkedIn Learning:** Offers thousands of professional development courses in business, marketing, leadership, time management, and more. These courses can help you build new skills or reinforce the ones you've already developed.

→ **Coursera:** Provides online courses from top universities like Yale, Stanford, and the University of Michigan. Consider courses in leadership, communication, project management, or other areas that align with your career interests.

→ **Udemy:** A platform with affordable courses on a wide range of topics including business, entrepreneurship, and software skills. Many courses are taught by industry experts.

→ **Project Management Certification (PMP):** If you're interested in project management, a PMP certification can be an excellent way to show potential employers that you have the skills to lead teams, manage timelines, and oversee successful projects.

→ **Google Analytics Certification:** If you're interested in marketing or data analysis, the Google Analytics certification will equip you with valuable skills for tracking and interpreting data.

→ **HR Certifications (e.g., SHRM-CP, PHR):** If human resources is an area of interest, consider certifications that will make you stand out as someone well-versed in HR practices and compliance.

Professional Organizations for Former Athletes

Professional organizations can be an invaluable resource for former athletes as you navigate your career transition. These organizations provide access to job opportunities, networking events, mentorship, and skill development. Here are some key organizations to consider joining:

- → **The National Association of Colleges and Employers (NACE):** Provides resources for college students and alumni, including job boards, networking opportunities, and career services. They often work with companies that value the transferable skills athletes bring to the table.

- → **The Professional Athletes' Career Transition Program (PACT):** Offers services to retired professional athletes, providing career counseling, resume building, job search strategies, and networking opportunities. PACT helps athletes transition from sports to careers in business.

- → **Athletes for Business (AFB):** A community that connects former athletes with businesses looking for individuals who possess skills like leadership, teamwork, and discipline. AFB provides networking, mentoring, and job placement opportunities.

- → **The Sports Industry Networking & Career Conference (SINC):** Aimed at students and alumni interested in working in the sports industry, SINC brings together employers, sports organizations, and aspiring professionals.

- → **Women's Sports Foundation (WSF):** Provides career resources and mentorship specifically for women athletes transitioning from sports to other industries. They also focus on empowering women in leadership roles.

CAREER TRANSITION SERVICES

If you're looking for more structured support as you transition, there are several career transition services specifically designed for former athletes. These services offer coaching, resume writing, interview preparation, and job placement assistance:

→ **Transition Coach:** Career coaches specializing in helping athletes transition into civilian careers. They offer personalized guidance, including resume building, interview preparation, and job search strategies.

→ **Upwork and Freelance Platforms:** If you're considering freelance or entrepreneurial work, platforms like Upwork or Fiverr can help you get started in fields like marketing, writing, consulting, and design.

→ **Veteran and Athlete Job Fairs:** Many organizations host job fairs specifically for veterans and athletes, where employers actively seek candidates with athletic backgrounds. These events provide a great opportunity for direct interviews and networking.

ADDITIONAL READING AND RESOURCES

While this book provides a strong foundation for your career transition, there are many other resources you can explore for ongoing career development. Consider these books and websites:

→ **"The Athlete's Guide to Career Transition" by Roberta B. Chinchilla:** This book focuses on helping athletes transition to life after sports, offering insights into career planning, job search strategies, and self-assessment.

→ **"What Color Is Your Parachute?" by Richard N. Bolles:** A classic guide to job-hunting and career change, this book offers practical tools for self-inventory, networking, interviewing, and discovering meaningful work that fits your unique talents and values.

→ **"The Art of Work" by Jeff Goins:** This book is about discovering your calling and aligning your passions with your work, helping you craft a career path that aligns with your strengths.

→ **CareerOneStop:** Sponsored by the U.S. Department of Labor, this website offers tools for job searching, resume building, and career exploration.

KEEP SHOWING UP, GIVING YOUR ALL, AND PLAYING TO WIN

This book has given you a powerful set of tools to succeed in the corporate world and beyond. But knowledge alone is not enough. The key lies in putting these skills into action every single day. Every time you lead with discipline, grow through challenges, communicate with purpose, or show resilience under pressure, you move one step closer to your goals.

You've already done what many never will. You've shown up early, stayed late, pushed through doubt, and kept going when things got tough. That strength lives in you now. Carry it into every challenge, every opportunity, and every new beginning. You are more than ready. You are built for this.

You are not just an athlete. You are a leader, a competitor, and a difference maker. Let your story speak for itself. Let your work show the world who you are. Success is not just about titles or trophies. It is about showing up with purpose, growing through adversity, and lifting others as you climb. You already know how to do that. You have been doing it your whole life.

Your journey from athlete to professional is just beginning. By leaning on your strengths and seeking out new opportunities to grow, you are equipped to make a powerful impact. The skills you built through sport are not just relevant in the workplace—they are your advantage.

Now take what you've learned. Believe in what you've earned. And step into what's next with confidence. You've got everything you need. Now go make it count.

You've got this!

ABOUT THE AUTHOR

Dr. Armin McCrea-Dastur is a seasoned leadership strategist and performance consultant with over thirty years of experience driving growth and transformation across business, healthcare, education, corrections, and sport. Her consulting and academic work consistently deliver measurable impact through strategic consultation, leadership development, and human capital transformation..

Dr. McCrea-Dastur's expertise bridges organizational change and performance psychology, with specialties in organizational design, change management, DEI (Diversity, Equity, and Inclusion), talent management, leadership development, and executive coaching. She has partnered with Fortune 500 companies, healthcare systems, universities, correctional institutions, and competitive athletic programs, working with C-level executives, frontline teams, and athletes at both amateur and professional levels to elevate performance and culture.

With a lifelong passion for athletics, she has built a distinctive niche at the intersection of business leadership and sport performance. She has collaborated with high-profile athletic programs, including work with Carolina Basketball, and continues to consult with collegiate athletes and teams to enhance mental toughness, focus, and resilience. In academia, she serves as Adjunct Faculty in the School of Business at the University of Connecticut, where she also contributes to the university's athletic department, and as Adjunct Faculty in the Psychology Department at Purdue University Global, bringing her dual background in leadership and sport psychology directly into the classroom.

Dr. McCrea-Dastur holds a Ph.D. in Organizational Leadership from The Chicago School of Professional Psychology, along with graduate degrees in Industrial/ Organizational Psychology and Sport Psychology. She is recognized by *Marquis Who's Who* for her career achievements and is widely regarded for her ability to integrate leadership science with practical strategies that drive individual and organizational excellence—whether in the boardroom, the classroom, or on the court.

CHAPTER 1:
The Bridge between Sports and Corporate Success

_____

_____

_____

_____

_____

_____

_____

_____

_____

_____

_____

_____

CAREER PLAYBOOK

CHAPTER 2:
Top Skills Corporate Leaders Look for in Candidates

_____

_____

_____

_____

_____

_____

_____

_____

_____

_____

CHAPTER 3: Discipline

_____

_____

_____

_____

_____

_____

_____

_____

_____

_____

_____

_____

CHAPTER 4: Time Management

_____

_____

_____

_____

_____

_____

_____

_____

_____

_____

_____

_____

CAREER PLAYBOOK

CHAPTER 5: Strategic Thinking

_____

_____

_____

_____

_____

_____

_____

_____

_____

_____

_____

_____

CHAPTER 6: Communication

_____

_____

_____

_____

_____

_____

_____

_____

_____

_____

_____

_____

CHAPTER 7: Leadership

_____

_____

_____

_____

_____

_____

_____

_____

_____

_____

_____

_____

CHAPTER 8: Teamwork

_____

_____

_____

_____

_____

_____

_____

_____

_____

_____

_____

CHAPTER 9: Emotional Intelligence

_____

_____

_____

_____

_____

_____

_____

_____

_____

_____

_____

_____

CHAPTER 10: Competitive Drive and Work Ethic

_____

_____

_____

_____

_____

_____

_____

_____

_____

_____

_____

_____

CHAPTER 11: Adaptability and Coachability

_____

_____

_____

_____

_____

_____

_____

_____

_____

_____

_____

CHAPTER 12: Resilience

_____

_____

_____

_____

_____

_____

_____

_____

_____

_____

_____

_____

CHAPTER 13: Bringing It All Together

_____

_____

_____

_____

_____

_____

_____

_____

_____

_____

_____

_____

www.ingramcontent.com/pod-product-compliance
Lightning Source LLC
Chambersburg PA
CBHW071209210326
41597CB00016B/1745